Just Rights

Just Rights

Bhuwan Ribhu

Published by
PRABHAT PRAKASHAN PVT. LTD.
4/19 Asaf Ali Road,
New Delhi-110 002 (INDIA)
e-mail: prabhatbooks@gmail.com

ISBN 978-93-5521-607-6
JUST RIGHTS
by Shri Bhuwan Ribhu

Edition
First, January 2024
Second, September 2024
Third, January 2026

Paperback Price
₹ 300.00 (Rupees Three Hundred only)

Printed at
R-Tech Offset Printers, Delhi

For the children, and their parents, who continue to wait in police stations and courtrooms, for justice.

For the children, and the parents, whom the system could not persuade to find the voice and the faith to come forward, and seek justice.

For my parents, whose life and work is a lesson in compassion and rights.

For my son, whose questions and thoughts everyday raise the dream of being just, and his Mama who continues to guard the dream.

For Chris, whose consciousness and life epitomizes love and justice.

Contents

On a cold November night, my 8-year-old son asked me how the universe came into being. I asked him, "What do you think?"

He replied, "Out of a 'Big Bang'. But what was there before the 'Big Bang'?" Then, I narrated to him this story:

"Once upon a nought, there was God. And God was.

Then God had a feeling. And that feeling was love.

As love came into being, love needed equilibrium and order. And this order was Justice.

Love and Justice came into being as the will of God, and time was created as the first born.

So God was 'just right' in His creation and in His order.

And, all the universes and multiverses continue on this path of just being and being just. Day or night, gravity, distance, proximity and expansion, all and everything, is in balance, and is just right.

The rest of it, is just our feelings and thoughts, and our stories."

As I was putting him to sleep, he asked me, "Then aren't we all just star people".

"Yes, we must be", I replied and as he slept, I thought about Love and Justice.

Being Just

This is a call of justice, and a call for justice.

This is an ode to a lot of 'just rights' coming together that make us all, and a demand for where we need to do more actions 'just right'.

What is Justice?

Any answer to this question that lays down any one definition will create a boundary that would be, and would need to be questioned, with time. Any attempt to limit it to the rule of law would invariably end up being a limitation. This would contribute more to the aporia than to the infiniteness of thought, insight and value of justice that is continuously evolving in the universe.

Humanity, with all its depth of knowledge, understanding and evolution, has yet not been able to crack the code of ensuring justice for all. Justice, that is understood only as 'access', or 'legal aid' or in various 'theories' is even further from being realised. At its narrowest interpretation, justice is about crime and punishment. When even this narrowest interpretation of justice – crime and punishment – is not achieved, then the individual and the society remain devoid of security, freedom, peace and justice, at the very least.

Though my experiences are mostly from India, I believe what India has achieved in policy formulation and social justice is a lesson for the world. Despite being a young nation with limited resources, high population, illiteracy and other such challenges, India has been able to convert each of its adversities into an opportunity, while overcoming diversities of cultures, religions, languages, to create one of the most robust, dynamic and holistic legal systems in the world.

Throughout India in the last 25 years, I have endeavoured to study and understand law from the eyes of the most marginalised, the most downtrodden and the worst affected people. In my interactions with them I have discovered that law alone is sometimes insufficient to ensure justice. This is even more true for the people who are victims of crime.

As sexual abuse of children is an anathema to the notion of being just, and of justice in any society, fighting for the rights of exploited and abused children and ensuring justice for them and their families, is the purpose of my life's work.

Till today[1], parents of the children who were killed in the Nithari village near Delhi in 2005-06[2], do not know who killed their children.

We have the best of intentions, laws and legal

1. January 2024
2. More details on Nithari tragedy follow

systems. Even the burden of proof in crimes like child sexual abuse is on the accused. Still, we continue to live in a society where in 2022, out of 268,038 cases, people accused of sexual crimes against children were convicted in only 8,909 cases – a mere three per cent of the total, while 243,000 cases are still continuing.

Why have we not been able to convert the ideals of laws framed in our Parliament, into deliverables for all on the ground? This is due to a combination of several factors.

Firstly, laws need to be amended with urgency in situations where they are needed and do not exist, or are insufficient.

Second, rampant lack of accountability is rooted in the interrelationship between the society and the State, where citizens do not follow law and order unless forced, and the State, being in a situation of authority, seeks to govern or rule, rather than to serve.

The State machinery, especially law enforcement and the judiciary, at various stages of the legal process, are often not answerable or accountable in practice for its acts or omissions. The laws framed by the legislature and judgments of higher courts, are the basis of policy and its implementation, and when not enforced, they continue to remain only on paper.

Third, delays in justice delivery result in a trust deficit in society that causes a vicious circle that needs to be broken. It is not merely a delay in the trial process but at all stages – from the formulation of laws themselves, to the identification of crimes in laws, to registration of existing crimes, medical, social and other processes for the rehabilitation and reparation of victims, to pending appeals of undertrials, to children being lodged in jails, to long delays before the High Courts and the Supreme Court, to lack of laws prescribing a timeframe for the completion of the entire process, etc.

Fourth, while there is an innate respect for justice that exists in Indian society as a part of *dharma,* a way of righteousness, over time, this respect is dwindling in practical application of laws. If laws are implemented improperly, judgements of courts are overlooked with impunity and people get away with murder, literally and figuratively, a sense of disillusionment and desensitisation arises in the society that challenges the very notion of rights and justness.

What is required is an intrinsic change in the perception of justice. For example, in India, 'Justice' is limited to "social justice, political justice and economic justice" as declared in the Preamble of the Constitution. "Ensuring access to justice" is a responsibility of the State as a part of Directive Principles of State Policy.

This understanding needs to evolve into a highly responsive reality that is felt and exercised by the individuals in the society.

In the overall functioning of the society, it is pertinent to look at the contribution of every person to maintain the equilibrium of justness. Is our role confined to follow the laws and enable the institutions to work smoothly? Or should we go a step further and use our moral compass to become responsible citizens? What about situations where we know that we will not be caught if we break the law, or where we are in a position of power which allows us to misuse our authority without oversight? The onus here is on each one of us.

Fundamentals of justice exist within us all and it is time that we change our relationship with ourselves, as individuals and as a society and that we exercise these fundamentals not only as a duty but also as a right.

In the past, I have often questioned myself, 'Is justice found only in the Constitution or books of laws? Is justice found only in the courts of law? Is justice found only in the policies or the institutions? Or, is justice a value, a feeling like love, undefined yet present in the souls of all humans?'

It is only now that I have learnt that justice is a path, a journey and a constant evolution of the human spirit. Justice is to be found; it is to be discovered. If it is to be realised, it must be a translation of the spirit of equilibrium, of righteousness, of morality and of the spirit of justness that exists within all of us.

As I share some of my experiences and struggles in trying to secure justice for thousands of victims of abuse and exploitation, I see that each of these cases or incidences is not a case file. It represents the hopes and dreams of children and parents who continue to put their faith in each one of us in the society that someday they will get justice. That hope, that dream lives on and so does the fight and fire for justice!

This book is also about some of the heroes who have fought this good fight and have walked on this fire path – a path that is a choice to act in the faith of what one believes to be just – beyond biases and the differences that are found in predetermined rights or wrongs. A path that is not driven by greed of today, but which can foresee the losses of tomorrow.

These heroes are the real harbingers of justice and they continue to exist amongst us, though often in the shadows. From an Assistant Sub Inspector of Police to some of the most well-known lawyers, to a former Chief Justice of India, to the nameless and faceless masses coming out of the comforts of their homes onto the streets to demand justice, I have tried to showcase what one action of a police person, or one judgement, or one step on this path can do to bring justice into the lives of millions. These actions are also mostly not known to the society at large and often these people themselves may not realise the consequences of their actions and yet continue to do what they hold to be just in the interest and service of others.

Beyond all notions of laws and courts, at some level there is such a hero in all of us. All of us – in our minds and sometimes in our actions - fight for the other person whom we do not know, fight for what we believe is right and what we believe is 'just' in society.

The arc of our righteousness, morality and our justness may be different, but it does exist. This justness in the spirit and soul that exists in each one of us, requires a space, a voice or an expression in our everyday actions. The evolutions of science, technology, communication and our intellect, have to contribute to our evolution as a species – an evolution of our consciousness that moves towards an equitable path of being fair, being righteous, being just.

This path of an amalgamation of thoughts and actions that arise out of love and justness is 'Justivism'.

'Justivism' is the pursuit and path for humanity to love and to serve, to nurture and grow, walk together not by force but by choice. To be just.

This is an endeavour to kindle this spirit of 'justivism' in all. And as those people who practice the thoughts, act in the spirit and in a manner that is more equal and fair, I have proposed one practical deliverable – Justice as a Fundamental Right.

At the core of this, is a belief and faith that we can change the way things are. While crime in some ways exists as a face of 'evil' in society, most laws exist as a face of the 'good' that is fighting this evil. This fight between good and evil continues. And shall exist with time. Though I am a believer, I do not think that crime will completely end in the world, but the impunity can, and will.

This idea is an attempt to side with, and assist, the good that is in each one of us, and in the world, on this path. This is a dream, a hope and a prayer to create this just world.

Many years ago, one of the most learned people in ancient scriptures in India had asked me whether God is inanimate or conscious? Without having learnt much about scriptures or ancient knowledge, I had responded, "The God there is, would be both, and would be in both."

The same, I believe, holds true for Justice.

1

Do you want law or do you want justice?

Law gives birth to crime.

Without a law defining an act as a crime, the act continues to remain just a moral wrong.

When there is no law, law should be made. When the law is insufficient in the pursuit of justice, it should be amended. Where the law itself does not achieve the end goal of justice, it must be repealed.

"What do you want? Law, or justice?", Assistant Sub Inspector (ASI) of Delhi Police, Paramjeet Singh asked me sitting in a dimly lit room on a chilly evening in the Civil Lines police station, North Delhi, on 21st November, 2005.

The day had begun with plans to celebrate the birthday of Vivek Tyagi, my friend from the Faculty of Law, Delhi University. Vivek and I had worked together to set up Save the Childhood Foundation (SCF), an organisation to combat trafficking and child labour as criminal justice issue.

Vivek was supposed to come over and spend the day with me.

While having my essential morning tea, an unusual news item in The Hindu newspaper caught my attention – one of the biggest operations by the Labour Department of Delhi Government to rescue child labourers, was planned to be conducted that day. The aim was to rescue hundreds of children from over 100 factories, with a plan to shelter and house over 2,000 rescued children. I wondered why the government would announce something like this in the media and still hope for it to be a success.

I was also interested in this operation as under my leadership, SCF had just undertaken a first of its kind of research on trafficking for child labour in Delhi, with the aim to establish that a majority of the children found working in the capital were victims of trafficking for forced labour and many other crimes. This was also a time when child labour was still a non-cognizable offence, with no police liability to register a case and trafficking itself not yet an offence.

Therefore, there was no question of any action against the traffickers, and the employers of child labour also went scot-free in most such cases. Through the research, I wanted to establish that while child labour remained a non-priority for the police, in a majority of instances of child labour, the children were also victims of many other crimes including, kidnapping, abduction, bonded labour or slavery, unlawful compulsory labour, etc., which were all punishable offences. Thus, I wanted to make a strong case for inclusion of trafficking of children, especially for forced labour, in the Indian Penal Code 1860 (IPC)[3] against which there was no specific law.

Till the law was made, I was advocating for the police to act in all cases of child labour and trafficking, under various other laws, prosecuting every one starting from the source areas from where the children were being procured by traffickers to the destination areas where the children were being employed. I also wanted to establish trafficking as an economic offence where the entire chain of demand and supply needed to be prosecuted and the money trail to be identified and illegal profits attached to create any deterrence.

So I called up my other colleagues who were involved in child labour rescue operations in the city, working with Bachpan Bachao Andolan (BBA), India's leading child rights organisation. BBA was also a member of the

---

3. Indian Penal Code was the official criminal code of India. In December 2023, it was replaced by Bharatiya Nyaya Sanhita or BNS

task force formed for the elimination of child labour in Delhi. As our research had suggested that the only place in the city where such a large number of children could be found working was in northeast Delhi, along with a couple of colleagues, I just decided to leave for that area and plan along the way.

On the way, we called up a number of BBA activists working in the area to confirm any such operation. Within the next few minutes, the BBA activists Salma Begum *ji*[4] and Sunil Trivedi *ji* reached the spot and confirmed our assumption that there was huge police deployment at Gonda Chowk in northeast Delhi.

The age-old wisdom of having 'boots on the ground' was paying off. The real success of any grassroots intervention is in the effective intelligence collection and swift response of the people on the ground. Huge organisations, movements and political parties, all owe their success to the tireless spirit, selfless service, dedication and sacrifices made by such foot soldiers. The leaders get the recognition and credit but sustainability of any social movement is primarily in the love, mutual respect and transfer of ideas and values between the various levels of decision making. And unless it is felt in the hearts, minds and actions of all, even the biggest organisations are destined to fail.

These activists form the cells of the body of the anti-child labour movement in the world, and it was their hard work and immediate response that contributed to an important milestone in the history of child rights in the days to come.

4. "*ji*" is a suffix used in the Indian subcontinent to give respect

On our way, we had also asked another lawyer friend from the Law Faculty, and co-founder of SCF, Raj Kumar Chandiwal, who was present in a nearby court, to join and help us.

When we arrived in the neighbourhood, we were astonished to see the level of preparation undertaken by the Delhi Police and the Labour Department. I counted more than 50 buses and other vehicles on the spot. The area had been cordoned off and they were combing each house in the locality in search of child labourers. We also joined in and started assisting the team.

Children were found to be working in most identified locations in illegally operating *zari* (garment embroidery) sweatshops in despicable conditions. Most were only 10 – 14 years old boys and were found to be wearing tattered clothes at the onset of Delhi winter.

Once the operation was completed, the rescued children were taken by the police and the Labour Department officials to Shastri Park, an open ground near the banks of the Yamuna river. Other government officials, media persons and employers of these children also joined in.

Over 450 children had been rescued (we later found it was 487) in possibly one of the largest rescue operations for trafficked child labourers in the world. The scenes at the Park were unimaginable. Angry employers were arguing and fighting with the labour department officials to let go of the children. According to them, the children had all come from Bihar or other states to work willingly in Delhi due to their poverty.

I just could not comprehend how, in the presence of the police and all these government officials, an employer or a trafficker had the audacity to claim that he was employing all these children, and still no action was being taken against him.

Unable to remain quiet in this situation, I started arguing with the police and the Labour Department officials, including the then Joint Commissioner, Piyush Sharma *ji*, asking them why were they not arresting the men who were admitting to have employed children in their factories and shops. They said it was not possible because child labour was a non-cognizable offence. I countered by saying that the authorities could press charges under the Bonded Labour System Abolition Act, 1986, or the Juvenile Justice (Care and Protection of Children) Act or JJ Act, 2000.

Within no time, it became a heated argument and journalists too joined in, asking the officials present and interviewing me on this issue. I climbed on top of my car and started addressing the media. The main thrust of my intervention was that the police was turning a blind eye to the crime by not taking action against these employers who were confessing to their crime.

As expected, I was immediately asked to leave the spot or else they threatened to have me arrested on charges of obstructing a public servant in the discharge of his duty. I had to leave in disappointment, angst and anger.

The inadequacies of existing laws, combined with a lack of interest of the enforcement agencies to implement whatever little that existed, was on full display. Instead of the planned 2,000, only 487 children were rescued from worst forms of trafficking and slavery and yet, no one was held guilty of anything!

It was around 2 pm. I called Vivek, who was now waiting for me at home and told him that I would join him in an hour.

*****

After about ten minutes of leaving, we received a phone call from one of the journalists whom we had just met at Shastri Park. He had called to inform that a complaint regarding a girl who was heard crying on the rooftop of a house at Rajpur Road. In all other circumstances, maybe the simple case of a child crying would have been forwarded to Childline services or the police. But that day, by some providential intervention, the universe had given us a chance to be of service.

On reaching the address we found the flat locked, and met the public spirited neighbour who had reported the matter to a journalist she knew. As we could not enter the house, we chose to go to the adjacent rooftop to investigate ourselves.

After jumping from the terrace of the neighbour's house on to the roof of the house from which the cries were heard, all we could see initially was a pile of clothes lying beneath a wooden cot. When I called out to see if someone was there, the pile of clothes moved. It was a girl who came out from under the cot, without any clothes on her, and as she took a couple of steps, she collapsed and became unconscious. She seemed about 12-years old. Her swollen face and more than 100 odd bruises all over her back told a tale of abuse and torture I had never witnessed before. Some of the wounds had dried blood on them, pus was oozing from others.

My first thought was that she was about to die.

I covered her with my jacket and called the police. Since it was a government colony, the Police were swift to act. A police team, led by Assistant Sub Inspector Paramjeet Singh, arrived at the spot within five to seven minutes. First, he admonished me and asked what I was doing there. When I pulled aside my jacket from the child, Singh saw the child and stepped back to gather himself.

Singh suggested that we immediately take the girl, Anjali[5] to nearby Aruna Asif Ali hospital. We reached the hospital in the next ten minutes and took the child to the emergency ward, where a doctor took charge of her. With that, we went out for a cup of tea. When we returned, we found the child on a stretcher, lying outside the hospital gate. She was still unconscious. When we turned to the doctors, they told us that the child was fit and we could take her back. We immediately picked a fight with the doctors saying how could we take the child when she was still unconscious?

In the meantime, an argument ensued. The local SHO (Station House Officer is the head of local police station) arrived. He began by chiding and questioning me when Paramjeet Singh intervened and took him aside and discussed something. When they returned, the SHO asked me to go and lodge an FIR (First Information Report is the registration of a criminal prosecution by the police and the beginning of the legal process) within

5. Name changed to protect identity

the next half hour, beyond which he would not be able to help us.

*****

I have been involved in legal actions fighting for the rights of children and other vulnerable sections of the society over the last two decades, with the police or other law enforcement or judicial officers. I have spent countless hours in police stations waiting for some police person to act in crimes against children. I have opposed police action, or inaction, before courts in scores of cases. I have been beaten black and blue by traffickers in the presence of the police who watched and did nothing.

Yet, I believe firmly, that it is the Police that are really responsible for law, order and protection in the society. The police are truly the real face of governance and as the first step in the legal system, their responsibility and empathy is quintessential in any endeavour to ensure protection to individuals and initiate the process of legal justice.

*****

The Police continues to work under all sorts of pressures, and while I do not know why the SHO that day said what he did, we left the girl with the SHO and Raj Kumar at the hospital. Paramjeet and I immediately left for the Civil Lines police station.

While drafting the complaint, Singh asked me which section of law should be invoked.

I was young, idealist and arrogant. And the events of the morning had brought me to a mental state where I believed that the police would hold that they had no role or jurisdiction in cases of child labour and would not act. So I told Singh I was not aware if this was a case of offences like hurt or causing grievous hurt as we were oblivious of the nature and extent of the child's injuries. We had still not spoken to the girl to ascertain if it was a case of bonded labour. Domestic child labour was not yet a part of the list of hazardous occupations and processes in which child labour was prohibited.

"Child labour is a non-cognizable offence so police cannot even register an FIR," I said.

The third option was a rarely used section (Section 26) of JJ Act, 2000. According to this section, whoever ostensibly procures a child or a juvenile for the purpose of any hazardous employment, keeps him in bondage and withholds the earnings of the child or uses such earnings for his own purposes, is punishable with up to three years and fine.

I told Singh that even if the girl was a domestic child labour, it was not possible to register a case under Section 26 of the JJ Act because child labour was not a hazardous employment.

"And why is domestic work not hazardous?" asked Singh.

"The list of hazardous jobs in the Child Labour Act does not mention domestic help," I responded.

"Who says that the word hazardous under the JJ Act has to be interpreted in line with the list given in the Child Labour Act?" he argued.

I responded, "It does not, but the law is ambiguous on the issue so the FIR can not be registered."

"**Do you want law or do you want justice**?" he retorted.

These words hit me with a sudden revelation that has had an indelible effect on me all these years. In some ways I have tried to live by this philosophy and have been guided by it.

He continued, "Interpreting the law is for the judge, not for us. Our job is to ensure that this child gets justice and the culprits are prosecuted".

The complaint was received and Paramjeet Singh and I returned to the hospital to discover that Anjali had regained consciousness. We took her to the police station. The FIR had been registered under Section 26 of the JJ Act, which was perhaps the first time that an FIR had been lodged under this section in India for domestic child labour. Paramjeet had invoked cognizable and non-bailable sections of the law and initiated action to arrest the employer.

I remember Singh ordering a portion of *daal* and mixed vegetables for the child and me, and one egg curry for himself, along with a dozen or so *rotis,* for dinner.

Singh and I went to freshen up and wash our hands while leaving the child in the room. As we returned, we found that the food had been delivered to the room and the little girl was hurriedly eating directly from the packet and foil. Within minutes, the child had eaten the food meant for three people as we stood at the door, watched her in silence with teary eyes. It was as if days or months of hunger were being fed.

Next, we contemplated where to take the girl. She could not have stayed at the police station and neither could I take her home without proper permissions, etc. This was also a time when India did not have a robust institutional framework for the care, safety and protection of children in need of care and protection that exists today. Around 10.30 pm, we took her to the nearby Missionaries of Charity Nirmal Hriday shelter home for destitute women and children. The staff, after much pleading, allowed the child to stay there overnight as she was to be produced before a court in the morning.

After dropping the little girl, and after calling up and apologising to Vivek for the umpteenth time that day, I left for home. As I drove back, I tried making sense of how Singh interpreted the law – justice is not a subject of law, and laws are there for the protection of justice. Singh had an innate sense of justice, which perhaps, I did not possess.

It was also clear that those in power were using loopholes in laws and institutions as justifications for their own inactions.

I met a visibly upset Vivek who gave me an earful for making him wait through the day and ruining his birthday. We ordered a pizza and as he was done venting, I told him I needed his help in drafting a public interest litigation (a public interest litigation, or PIL, is one of the strongest tools available for a person in India to approach a High Court of a state or the Supreme Court of India for enforcement of his or any other person's fundamental rights in larger public interest). He had experience in drafting such a writ petition or PIL, while I had none.

Vivek and I worked through the night, drafting a PIL to be filed before the High Court of Delhi regarding the rescue of 487 child labourers from Gonda Chowk. The PIL sought clear roles and responsibilities for different law enforcement agencies, why the police must act in a case of child labour and various other points for rescue and rehabilitation of children trafficked for forced labour.

The following morning, we were racing against time to finalise and file the petition. As the day progressed, the girl who had been rescued in the evening was produced before a magistrate to give her statement. Colleagues informed me that the court would give her custody only to a female and they had contacted my mother for the same.

At about 5 pm that evening, the landline at my office desk rang.

"Come downstairs. I'm waiting for you for lunch," said the female voice at the other end. I thought it was my mother. But that was not the time for lunch, and I was too engrossed in work, so I apologised and hung up.

The phone rang again.

"I have not eaten since morning. Come!" she said. I was a bit annoyed this time.

"I told you I'm busy. Go ahead and eat if you feel like," I disconnected the line.

The third time the phone rang and the voice said, "I will not eat if you will not come downstairs."

I then realised that it was not my mother. I enquired who she was.

"You think of yourself as a big shot lawyer and have forgotten me in a day?"

Sitting alone in my office, I started crying as I realised that it was the little girl - a child who I thought was going to die not 24 hours ago and whose name I still did not know. A child who had not spoken a word to me till then and had simply watched silently, as I had pleaded with folded hands the previous night before the shelter home manager to accommodate her for one night. A child who had gotten her life and her voice back. This was what freedom could do in half a day.

With tears in my eyes, I started walking from my fourth floor office to the nearby BBA office where the little girl was waiting for me to have a late lunch with her. While talking to her, I realised for the first time that her name was Anjali. And, for the second time in two days, I was wondering how little did I understand about justice, laws and rights.

What one night of freedom, one responsible citizen who reported a crying child and one proactive policeman could do to bring back to a 12-year-old child her life, a trust and a renewed faith in humanity and a smile on her lips! What one action could do to bring back the confidence of life itself.

From living a life of slavery and exploitation where she was kept without food for days, beaten with barbed wires, made to work without any clothes on, made to sleep on the roof, to being a child once again. All it took was 24 hours of 'justivism'.

Two days later, as I was entering the office, a man came and fell at my feet, crying. As I lifted him up, someone mentioned that he was the father of Anjali and had come from Chhattisgarh. I turned stone-cold out of anger and roughly told him to get out of my sight as he had sold off his daughter.

Then he told his story.

With tears streaming down his rough-hewn face, he said, "It is all because of English."

Thereafter he told that he was a policeman from Raigarh in Chhattisgarh and that he had sent the 11-year-old Anjali to his so-called brother from his village, to acquire better education. He believed that he had not risen enough in life because of a lack of English language skills and thought that his so-called village brother, who was a senior engineer in Delhi, would take care of his daughter and she would get better education that would enable her to speak in English. Over the next eleven months, he never even called once, believing that his daughter was doing fine. Little did he know of the life of torture, slavery and abuse his daughter would have to undergo.

If a policeman's daughter could be trafficked in the name of better education by a high-ranking government official, the level of awareness and deterrence against trafficking and child abuse was negligible in society.

Her father took Anjali home after a few days and it became one of the first (if not 'the first') cases of a trafficked domestic child labourer being rescued under the JJ Act 2000. It also became one of the first such cases resulting in a conviction.

I will never forget the meal I had with Anjali, or the question I was asked by ASI Singh, and it all started that day in 2005, with that one question –

Do you want law or do you want justice?

□

2

Lightning may also strike twice: Law must reach far and wide

In the emerging world of crime, laws are always following and catching up and defining crimes.

The notion or understanding of laws and their evolution need to constantly reflect upon the prevailing situation in the society and its ever-increasing requirements.

Laws need to be formulated on the basis that the macro – level policy must reach the micro – level citizen and the issues or problems of the citizen must guide the formulation and revision of macro – level policy.

On the night of 21st November 2005, when Vivek Tyagi and I had prepared the PIL, we had not imagined that it in the months to come, it would change the country's response mechanism on child protection.

From being only a poverty-driven social justice issue, trafficking of children for forced labour and child labour also became criminal justice issues, infested with organised crime.

The history of trafficking for the purpose of slavery or for sexual exploitation, is almost as old as the history of human civilisation. In India, the Constitution prescribed the Right Against Exploitation in 1950 as a Fundamental Right enshrined in Article 23 and Article 24.

Article 23 states: "Prohibition of traffic in human beings and forced labour.—(1) Traffic in human beings and *begar* and other similar forms of forced labour are prohibited and any contravention of this provision shall be an offence punishable in accordance with law."

While Article 24 states: "Prohibition of employment of children in factories, etc.—No child below the age of fourteen years shall be employed to work in any factory or mine or engaged in any other hazardous employment."

Despite these being constitutional mandates as Fundamental Rights, the trafficking of children for forced labour as well as child labour was not prohibited or explicitly defined as a crime.

For the first time, as a result of various orders, judgments and enhanced understanding of laws that became a precedent through this case, the law defining and prohibiting trafficking was made in 2013, and the law prohibiting child labour till the age of 14 years came into existence in 2016.

In 2006 itself, the Government of India banned the employment of children as domestic child labour and in *dhabas* (eateries) in India till the age of 14 (on 10th October, 2006). The same year, the High Court of Delhi directed the central government and Delhi state government that rehabilitation of children is the responsibility of the state and the state can-not abdicate from this responsibility by citing any NGO's initiatives.

The roles and responsibilities of all the government departments, especially for the police to act and prosecute employers and traffickers in child labour cases, were first affixed on 15th July 2009 in the same case filed us in November 2005. For the first time, child trafficking for labour was seen holistically and an ecosystem-level response was envisaged, including the role of principle employers. The Department of Education and the Municipal Corporation of Delhi were given responsibilities for prevention and ensuring access to education for all children. Police and Labour Department were tasked with the rescue of children and prosecution of employers. The Revenue Department was even empowered to recover fines from the employers as an arrear of land revenue, as a civil fine, even without conviction and use this amount for the rehabilitation of the rescued children.

The overall institutional framework that currently exists in India for rehabilitation and education in cases of trafficking and child labour can be attributed, to a large extent, to the changes brought about by the High Court in this case, reiterated and expanded further in other similar cases, and eventually leading to the laws on trafficking and the employment of children being overhauled.

Child labour was also defined for the first time, globally, in this case. All these developments paved the way for the eventual complete ban on child labour in India till the age of 14 years, and in hazardous occupations and processes till the age of 18 years, in 2016. What started as a strategic and angry response to the apathy of a few government officers laid the foundation for the prevention, protection, prosecution and rehabilitation of trafficked children for forced labour.

*****

While the recue and rehabilitation efforts began to take shape, in 2011, there was a raid by the police and Labour Department in Najafgarh, Delhi, in which 20 children were rescued from 19 *dhabas* (roadside eateries). All 19 employers of 20 child labourers deposited the mandatory fine of Rs. 20,000 each for the employment of children on the very day of the raid.

I had never seen this happen, so I went to these *dhabas* three days later, pretending to be a customer. As I ate or had tea at four of them, one after another, I asked their owners why they had deposited the fine.

As a part of my act, I even told one, "These NGO people are all corrupt and had rescued poor children from my brother's factory and we never paid a penny as fine."

The owner nonchalantly responded, "We will bring other children the next day and earn over Rs. 20,000 from them within two months. Who wants to waste time in courts and police stations? Better to pay and get it over with. As it is, lightning does not strike twice and who will come back now to check?"

I realised then that what these employers and traffickers wanted was, to save their time and money, rather than get entangled in court procedures away from their factories or shops.

For the employers, the fine or penalty was not a deterrent as they would continue to employ children and recover their lost money by using these unpaid or marginally-paid trafficked bonded labourers.

The parents, in most cases of trafficking, love their children and want them to have a better life. However, they are enticed or deceived into sending their children away, on the false promise or assurance of a better future, a skill or an education.

Whereas, for the traffickers, the child is a commodity to be sold and exploited, to be profiteered from again and again. For them it is all about the money.

There is no fear like the fear of the loss of something one loves. As trafficking is an organised crime, the only way to combat it was to hit the economics of it. When the cost of procurement and replacement would exceed the margins of profit, where an employer would have to pay back fines, and back wages as per the minimum wage law, as well as spend time, energy, effort and money on lawyers, police and courts, trafficking would stop.

I asked a lawyer friend, Anand Kumar, to do a background legal research on the issue. Anand has a bespectacled and frail look that belies his lion heart and spirit and knowledge of the law. A veteran of hundreds of child labour cases, he understood the issue and nailed the legal argument within a day. So we went back to the same case and filed a fresh application for the rescue of children and recovery of fines, back wages and attachment of properties as proceeds of crime. While a law may only look at a crime from the narrow lens of 'incidence', justice would be served in the entire chain of prevention, protection, prosecution, rehabilitation, identification of illegal profits and their attachments and reparation for the victim as well as for the society.

Eventually, the court directed the sealing of factories employing children, recovery of fines without conviction as an arrear of land revenue, recovery of back wages as per the minimum wages law and prosecution under stricter laws.

This is a learning for life I received that fateful day from the people who employed trafficked children at their eateries. I have always tried to impress this learning upon any person in law enforcement or judiciary or civil society I have had the honour of training or teaching.

Many times we do not attempt to take on a problem because we believe that the solution is impossible, or the problem is too big, or we are too small. Young activists, police officers, judges and others often take an issue head on because they do not have the baggage of knowledge, wisdom and experience that tells them that the problem is unsolvable. We took on this issue without knowing that it was impossible and hundreds of activists, police officers, lawyers and judges helped us, believing that it was the right thing to do.

*****

A policeman told me the following story years ago.

Lord Shiva, who was responsible for bringing the rain on Earth, decided to not dance for ten years. If He did not dance, there would be no rains. An announcement was made on earth and everyone was informed about

Lord Shiva's decision. Everyone stopped farming and cultivating the land considering all their efforts would be futile, in the event of no rains.

However, a curious Goddess Parvati decided to see for Herself how the farmers were coping with this change. To Her surprise, while all the farmers had stopped farming, there was one farmer who continued to work hard tilling his land.

When she approached him, he was too busy to notice Her. However, when he rested for lunch, he came to the Goddess with folded hands and apologised for his earlier behaviour.

Goddess Parvati asked him if he was aware of Lord Shiva's decision and that without rain, his efforts would all go in vain.

To this, the poor farmer replied, "Lord Shiva is the God. He can do as He pleases. If I do not do what I must if I do not do what is my dharma, I will forget how to till my land. He is God and He is forgiven everything, but if I forget my duty, Mother Earth will never forgive me."

Goddess Parvati went back to Lord Shiva and recounted the entire story to him. She said that the man on Earth was merely a farmer, yet he knew that he was supposed to follow his path irrespective of the outcome, and was well aware that he was not responsible for your actions, but for his own.

"He knows that he must do whatever he can whether you, the Lord, follow your dharma or not. Also, he is aware that if he does not do so, he would forget his dharma in ten years. Won't you?" Goddess asked Shiva.

Lord Shiva immediately realised his mistake and that he had deviated from his path of justice. He danced and it rained. Besides, not only did the farmer grow crops, but Lord Shiva also blessed him that on his land, he would have enough crops to feed the entire society.

The farmer continued to follow his path, his norm and his law. Meanwhile, when God himself did not follow his dharma, He was reminded and He returned to the path and the laws He had created Himself.

What that policeman's story taught me was that Lord Shiva is not only the Lord of rain; Lord Shiva is the Lord of justness, of order, of justice. Lord Shiva represents all of us and so does the farmer.

The expectations of result should not govern the action; it is the feeling of doing an action because it is the just thing to do. Justice is a thing to be practiced; justice is a path and not a destination and the society's end goal is to achieve justness. The path itself should be of justness.

*****

Most of the laws and policies that exist in the world today started with one person who decided to act in the interest of justice - beyond what existed, and not be bound by what is rather what can be. History is often written from the perspective of the victor, folklores and legends narrate the stories of the brave, of the just.

Step by step, if one works for justice, the laws will follow. If a law is not there, it will eventually be made. If the law is inadequate, it will eventually be amended. Follow the path of being just, the path of justice, and laws and policies will eventually find a way to be formed, or reformed. No problem is bigger than the will of the just. And many a times the young are brave because they do not realise that what they do is impossible to do.

I have learnt to always seek to be just. And just be. To be responsible, and take responsibility. No excuses. No justifications.

Towards justness, it is only your actions that matter and in these situations, it may literally be a life at stake. What is just another phone call for you in the world maybe the entire world to the person on the other end of that line.

10 Years Later

In 2023-24 alone, of the interventions that I was a part of in India, 29,224 trafficked children were rescued, 16,084 prosecutions were launched and 6,419 traffickers were arrested. To protect our girls from the crime and scourge of child marriage, NGOs' efforts resulted in over 75,000 child marriages being prevented. These are some of the 'just' interventions and efforts of over 161 NGOs to uphold the law and pormote the rule of justice. The real numbers of change throughout the country due to the efforts of police and other law enforcement agencies would be much higher.

And these are not merely numbers but children returning back to a world of possibilities, to their parents, back to their lives, back to their future!

□

3

Who killed our children?

"If we fail to protect our children, nothing else that we do in life matters."

There is a world of difference between law and justice.

Justice continues to evade millions of men, women and children in the absence of laws prescribing punishment, or laws that continue to remain inadequate or are not implemented, or laws and policies for which no accountability for inaction lie.

Justice also continues to evade everyone who continues to wait endlessly for it by going through the legal process that they do not even understand.

"A 'missing child' is not a 'kidnapped' child, and is not a crime. The police does not have to register a case. The law is clear. You can do whatever you want!" I was told after waiting for several hours at a Police station in 2006.

I was aghast and decided to approach the High Court and file a *Habeas corpus*[6] as I walked out of the police station. In the car, as my anger subsided, I wondered what would be the fate of the people who do not know what is available to them as a remedy in law.

'Law' is just a word; but is law always a 'just' word?

When the words and expressions in laws are interpreted in a manner that defeats its very purpose of providing protection and work against the spirit of the law itself, there is little recourse available.

It is the words that were used to take away the rights of the children who went missing in Nithari in 2006 – their right to be searched for; their right to be found; their right to be saved.

Words that were used and interpreted to take away the rights of the parents, who went to the police station over the years and asked for something as elementary as an effort to find and recover their missing children.

The cases were not registered or investigated by the police, for the simple reason of wordplay that each of these was a case of a 'missing child', and not of 'kidnapping'.

6. The writ of Habeas corpus is a mechanism available in law to have a person or a body brought before the court

Where can a parent go whose child is missing and who is not helped by the police citing a legal technicality in the usage of words? What does one do if the police follow only the law and the law is not enough to ensure justice?

Nithari is a name that keeps haunting the conscience of a generation in India that could read the newspapers in 2006. In 2024, it has also become one of the stark reminders of our collective colossal failure as a society to ensure justice, even if it means something as basic as conviction for the guilty.

It was in July 2006 that some parents were brought to my office for legal assistance because their children had gone missing. They were from a village in Noida, called Nithari, about 20 kms away from the Parliament and the Supreme Court of India, in New Delhi. About 38 children had gone missing from their village in the preceding year. Police were not registering many of these cases and had done nothing for their recovery.

In December 2006, children's body parts were found in a drain behind the house of one Moninder Singh Pandher, who lived with his domestic help, Surinder Koli. Both Pandher and Koli were promptly arrested, the case transferred to the Central Bureau of Investigation (CBI), India's premier investigating agency, and in time, both were convicted of their crimes and awarded the death sentence in various cases by the courts.

What is right and what is wrong may always be relative but there can be no excuse or justification for not searching for a missing child citing any legal technicality.

Police inaction making no attempt to trace and recover 38 missing children in a particular area was nothing but abject failure of everything that the rule of law stands for and the prime example of why only the rule of law is not enough.

After being awarded the death sentence in many cases, after having their mercy petition dismissed by the President of India in 2014, after 17 years, in 2023 both the accused persons of the Nithari killings were acquitted. For the parents, it was an agonising wait resulting in nothing.

A person who is innocent should not be condemned to his fate for 17 long years. Similarly, the victim should not have to wait. The parents are still looking for a closure, and a father whose missing son would have turned 20 this year can do nothing more than to throw a brick at the house where he continues to believe his three-year-old son was murdered.

This denial of justice leaves a void in society which questions our very notion of who we are and what we are striving for, individually as well as collectively. It also leaves behind an anger and a frustration that can only be expressed in acts of violence, or acts of depression, or both.

There is no system in place to deal with this situation. In our courts, somebody is convicted, somebody is acquitted and then the case is closed as if nothing has happened. None has been killed, and no one has killed them.

If the society had pursued the ends of justice, the case would remain open till the question is answered for the parents in Nithari in 2006: "Who killed our children?"

It is January 2024. It is four months since the accused have been acquitted. It is 17 years since the killings.

The children of Nithari, and justice, are still missing.

□

4

When a judge does not ask why, but asks why not: The presumption of crime

"A judge with his pen can alter the course of the future of the nation".

The real deterrence of law in society is not in the severity of punishment but in the certainty of it.

The Doctrine of Presumption of Crime is that in certain situations, it must be presumed that a crime has taken place and the onus of proving that the crime has not taken place is on the police.

Each year, over a hundred thousand children are saved because a judge decided to presume a crime.

In July 2006, when I met the parents of the children from Nithari, I believed it was a case of trafficking of children, for forced labour or sexual exploitation, kidnapped from poor parents.

With little pressure from the media or elsewhere, no influence, the hapless parents of these missing children were desperately seeking answers and hoping someone would help them find their missing children. The desolate parents were tormented by the 'what ifs' behind the disappearance of their children.

I tried to raise the issue before various forums in August – September 2006 while preparing a *habeas corpus* petition with the parents for the recovery of these children before the High Court of Allahabad.

This was also the time when Anjali's case had borne result and domestic child labour had been outlawed in India (on 10th July 2006 to come into effect from 10th October 2006). So many conferences were being organised by the civil society in Delhi over the issue of child labour.

In one such conference organised at the India International Centre in New Delhi by One World South Asia, I was invited to speak. As I raised the issue of the missing children of Nithari, a very senior police officer, who was also one of the speakers said, "A missing child is 'just' a missing child. It is neither an offence nor a crime and so the police is not duty-bound to act".

Besides brushing off the police's role in investing these missing children, he further said that these girls often "run away and elope with their boyfriends".

I was furious. I challenged him in the middle of the crowd if he would have had the audacity or the guts to use this language if it concerned the daughter of a politician or a corporate big shot. And I said such policemen were not fit to wear the pride of our nation, the symbol of our strength, the national emblem of our country, the Ashoka Pillar on their foreheads. I asked him to resign then and there.

He was also infuriated. I was politely asked to step down and leave the conference venue. I left the conference but now the journalists who were present raised the issue. In the next few days, many news articles appeared in the media about the missing children of Nithari, but to our anguish, no action was taken and the children remained missing.

Before the petition could be filed, in December 2006 the entire country shared the anguish and rage of the parents and the activists, as the parts of the bodies of over a dozen children were found in a drain with dogs eating them, behind the house of Moninder Singh Pandher, where he lived with his domestic help, Surinder Koli.

The nation had never been witness to such a horror. A high level committee was immediately constituted by the Central Government. The National Human Rights Commission (NHRC) took cognizance of the case in the first week of 2007, and one assumed that the issue of missing children would finally find its space and focus in policies and actions.

Later, in its report on the missing children, the Commission wrote, "The revelations at Nithari exemplify that missing children may end up in a variety of places and situations – killed and buried in a neighbour's backyard, working as cheap forced labour in illegal factories/establishments/ homes, exploited as sex slaves or forced into the child porn industry, as camel jockeys in the Gulf countries, as child beggars in begging rackets, as victims of illegal adoptions or forced marriages, or perhaps worse than any of these as victims of organ trade and even grotesque cannibalism, as reported at Nithari."

But as days went by and the anger subsided, we realised that nothing much was changing.

In 2008, I was one of the National Secretaries of BBA and with limited financial and human resources at our disposal, my colleagues and I tried to ascertain the nature and extent of the issue of missing children in India. We filed applications under Right to Information Act (RTI) in each district of India and asked every police station how many children were reported to be missing under their jurisdiction.

The data on missing children was painstakingly collected over the next three years. Most police stations failed to respond the first time. The RTI applications were refiled and eventually data from 392 districts out of approximately 600 districts was collected and analysed for comparison with the data of registration of FIRs under kidnapping and related sections collected by the National Crime Records Bureau (NCRB).

In December 2011, (late) Justice Altamas Kabir, who was then a judge of the Supreme Court of India released the pioneering study of BBA titled, "Missing Children of

India". The data collected for the period January 2008 to January 2010 revealed that in the 392 districts, during that period, 117,480 children went missing as per the official police records. As many as 41,546 remained untraced while the NCRB figures showed that only 16,595 FIRs were registered throughout India under the sections of kidnapping.

Armed with this data, BBA approached the Supreme Court with a writ petition asking for compulsory registration of FIRs whenever a case of a missing child was reported. We also asked for immediate action by the police as the first few hours are most critical in the recovery of a missing child.

*****

In India, till 2013, missing children was an ever-growing problem with no apparent solution. If a child went missing, it was not a case of 'kidnapping'. In most such cases, poor and uneducated parents would approach the police and report that their child was 'missing'. Since no offence was made out for a 'missing child', the police would simply make an entry in their General Diary (GD), which is their daily log of incidents or interactions within the police station's jurisdiction.

In case a parent would write in the complaint that their child had been kidnapped, the local police would ask if they knew who could have kidnapped the child. If the parents were to reply "no", the police would ask them to simply write in their complaint that the child had gone missing. God forbid, if the missing child was a girl of over 12 -13 years, then the first response of the police personnel would invariably be, *"ghar ja, kisi ke saath bhaag gayi hogi"* (Go home, she must have run off with somebody). The poor parents would then be faced with the ignominy as well as the fear for their missing child.

In most cases, the parents would not know the difference between an FIR and a General Diary entry and no investigation would be launched to trace the missing child after a General Diary entry.

In 2003, the National Human Rights Commission (NHRC) reported that over 45,000 children went missing in India while only about 2,500 FIRs were registered. In 2013, this number increased to over 135,000 with around 28,000 FIRs.

Considering that the poorest of the poor and people living in far-off tribal areas, or mines or remote mountains or forests do not even report a missing child, the real number may even be more. But what these numbers reflected was also extremely frightening.

When we approached the Supreme Court of India in 2010, every hour, 11 children were reported missing and only one was being searched for by the police. To protect the rest, who were 'missing' and not 'kidnapped', there was no law.

There is no bigger helplessness and no bigger hopelessness than what is felt by parents when their child goes missing. This is worsened where there is no help forthcoming from anywhere.

Even worse is the fate of justice when all the Constitutions and law books, and policies and theories of justice are futile before the tears of a mother who has reported the crime of her missing child. She, who has continued to wait in faith but in vain, unaware that no one is looking for her child.

It is true that the onus of imparting justice to the most marginalised is on the powerful; the entrusted. The people who know the law and can act. Above all else, people who can stretch the boundaries of what exists through their statesmanship, leadership, wisdom and vision.

Former Chief Justice of India, Mr Altamas Kabir (centre) walking on the streets of Guwahati to spread awareness against trafficking in 2012.

India was fortunate to have in Justice Altamas Kabir, a hero whose actions saved over a hundred thousand missing children each year, with a stroke of a judgement that pushed the boundaries of law and justice in India, and the world, and laid down the Doctrine of Presumption of Crime.

Before this, like in Nithari, a missing child's case was not even registered and investigated by the police.

*****

As the case for compulsory registration of FIRs in all cases of missing children was being heard, the country witnessed another horror in the brutal rape and murder of a young paramedic student that came to be known as the Nirbhaya rape case.

Once again, the country's collective conscience was shaken and people's anger came out on the streets. As a result, many changes in laws and policies were made. The students across the country, the young people and young India were on the streets, each resonating the horror, anger and anguish of the Nirbhaya rape case. These young people were the true catalysts of change. The Justice Verma Committee was formed by the government in the aftermath of their outrage and outpouring, post Nirbhaya rape case. The Committee, mandated to recommend amendments in the legal framework for protection of women from sexual violence, recommended in January 2013, that all missing children's cases should be compulsorily registered.

In January itself, the Supreme Court passed an order

in BBA's[7] case that in all cases of missing children FIRs should be registered. It was thought that this time the law enforcement agencies would become more responsive. But all the states raised the objection before the Supreme Court that the law and order situation would collapse and all cases of missing children could not be investigated.

In April 2013, a 5-year-old child went missing while playing near her house in Gandhinagar, Delhi. Police registered the case later that night and did little else. Knowing fully well that it was not a case where a contempt of court was made out, and we would fail, we approached the Supreme Court in the same missing children matter claiming that the Delhi Police Commissioner had committed a contempt of the Supreme Court's directions of January 2013 as the police had not acted properly.

We initiated this with the belief that if there was an application pending before the Supreme Court, the police would act promptly and would do everything to prove to the court that we were wrong. We were right.

The then Chief Justice of India, Hon'ble Mr. Justice Altamas Kabir saw through the ruse instantly when the application came before him. He smiled sadly. He took up the application along with all the states' objections.

I had gotten a first-hand glimpse of his empathy and love for children when his wife, Mrs. Mina Kabir had approached me, years earlier, to provide for shelter, education and medicines for a child in conflict with law. This child needed medicines for juvenile diabetes and

7. Writ Petition Civil 75/ 2012 - Bachpan Bachao Andolan vs Union of India and Others

would commit petty crimes so that he could be housed in an observation home where he would get free medicines.

Justice Kabir was a short, stout and soft-spoken man with a resolve of steel and a sense of humour that only he, or people close to him, understood. His love for children and justice resulted in an impetus and brought a spotlight on children's issues across the country during his tenure at the Supreme Court. His deep baritone voice and beaming smile and affectionate aura radiated a warmth that very few people in positions of power exude.

I realised it only after a few years that he had heard this case as of utmost importance and urgency, three times within two weeks, as the Supreme Court was going into summer break in mid-May and he was due to retire as soon as the courts reopened in July.

He wanted to ensure that he did justice to the cause and to the parents of the missing children. He heard all the arguments and the case at length over three hearings. While the contempt application was dismissed as withdrawn by us, the arguments made by the states and the central government against the compulsory registration of FIRs were heard.

*****

On 10th May 2013, led by Justice Kabir, the bench comprising Justice S. A. Bobde and Justice Vikramajit Sen, gave a landmark judgement. The states' objections were set aside and it was made compulsory for all cases of missing children to be registered. The police had to prove through investigation that the child had not been a victim of kidnapping or trafficking.

What the court laid down was the Doctrine of Presumption of Crime. In certain circumstances, it may be presumed that a crime has taken place even when there is no specific crime reported. The Court laid down the definition of who was a 'missing child' for the first time in the world. Institutional reforms were introduced in the appointment of para legal volunteers in all police stations, while the capacity and knowledge of police was enhanced by the Standard Operating Procedure for investigating missing children cases. It also mandated that all crimes against children have to be registered and investigated as per the law.

A three-page judgement of the Supreme Court dictated in open court without any frills, embellishments or quotes laid the foundation for the safety of hundreds of thousands children since then.

This one shift in legal interpretation of law towards justice has led to thousands of traffickers being arrested and over 100,000 children being saved annually from being trafficked or go missing.

*****

Many crimes and many criminals remain outside the ambit of law simply because the laws governing these crimes have been interpreted by the enforcement agencies mechanically and technically. A situation which is a crime, needs to be recognised as such.

If the police feign their inability to act because a crime does not exist in law, it results in a lack of access to justice for the victim who has not found recourse in the legal system. The onus or responsibility of ensuring that a crime is recognised as such, and the laws are interpreted in favour of the victims towards the ends of justice, is the responsibility of the people in positions of decision-making.

The underlying ideal is that true justice lies in the acts that are just, fair, promote equality and equilibrium, bring closure to the victims, ensure swift retribution, restitution and deterrence, thereby preventing crime and again conform justice in society.

Justice delivery is a process, which has to work at a number of stages with multiple people for it to be successful. At its very basic level, this process includes:

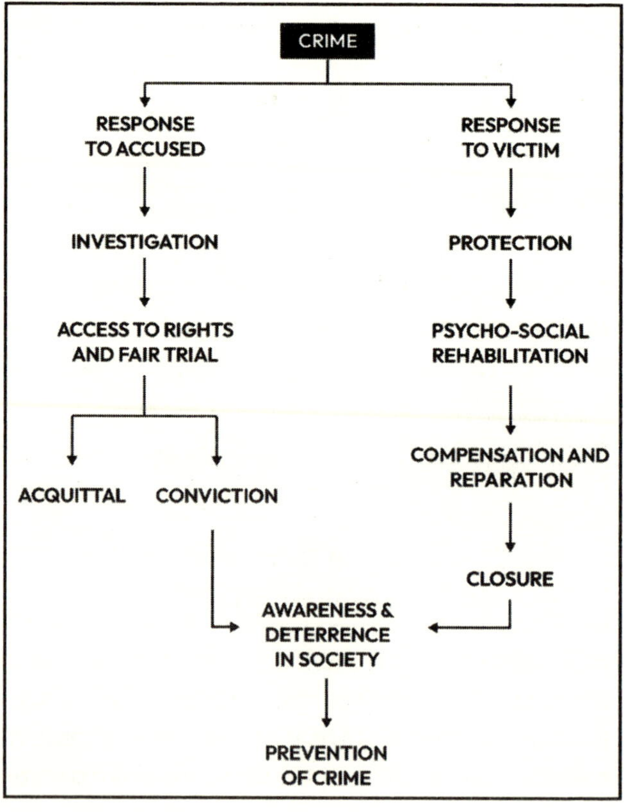

At every stage, the highly technical legal processes become mechanised in such a way that the more skilled a technician is, the better use he can make of the machine. Thus, the legal process tends to become skewed or aligned in favour of the lawyers, practitioners, or people who can make better sense or better interpretations of it.

A tool in the hands of a few automatically creates a power imbalance in society. More so, if the tool is of knowledge, or as in this case, an instrument for the delivery of something as inherent as justice.

The law should be for all, but in its formation, existence and dissemination, the law fails to reach out and create a trust in society in favour of its implementation. And the implementation of a law against crime is but a first step towards the delivery of justice.

*****

When the law for the protection of missing children came to be implemented in letter and spirit, in 2015, within a year of the oversight by the Supreme Court, the number of FIRs increased to 41,000 and the number of missing children in India fell down to 61,000.

In the same year, the compulsory registration of all child care institutions also became mandatory as a part of the Juvenile Justice (Care and Protection of Children) Act, 2015. This meant that all the children in child care institutions were accounted for. I had an idea to use technology for the recovery of missing children. If all the missing children photographs are on the same portal, and all the children being housed in Child care institutions could be photographed and matched with the missing children, maybe some missing children who may have been recovered and are housed in child care institutions could be traced.

I approached the Delhi High Court asking for an order to match the photographs of the missing children in India with the photos of the children housed in these child care institutions. In April 2018, the Delhi police matched these photos through the introduction of facial recognition software. Within a week, over 3,000 missing children were matched.

In the last decade, this Doctrine of Presumption of Crime became a cornerstone in jurisprudence, ensuring access to rule of law for all victims of trafficking, thus even contributing to safeguarding of Article 23 of the Constitution.

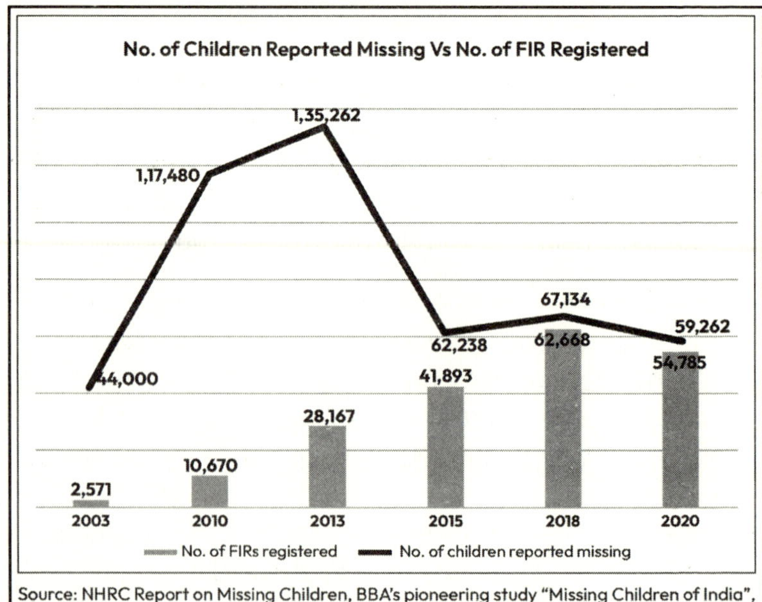

Source: NHRC Report on Missing Children, BBA's pioneering study "Missing Children of India", Response to Parliament Question and NCRB

The number of missing children increased from 45,000 in 2003 to 135,262 in 2013. Since then it has come down to 59,262 in 2020. During the same time, the number of FIRs registered for the crime of kidnapping have increased from 2,571 in 2003 to 54,785 in 2020, due to the Supreme Court judgement.

While it appears that the crime has increased multifold, in reality the number of missing children has actually reduced from 135,262 in 2013 to 59,262 in 2020– in a space of seven years.

Thus, it became clear that this increase in the number of FIRs registered was not an increase in crime. The crime always existed; it doubled even in reported figures in the ten-year period between 2003 till 2013.

The increase in registration of FIRs and subsequent identifications and arrests of kidnappers and traffickers meant that over a period of the subsequent seven years (post 2013), not only was this increase in crime rate arrested but the crime rate itself was reversed.

The number of children reported missing and continuing to remain untraced has, in fact, decreased and is coming down substantially.

The true test of the implementation of a law is in the impact of its deterrence. This is perhaps the best example in the world, of a legal deterrent resulting in justice through the prevention of crime.

And there is no better indicator of this impact than the smiling face of a child who did not go missing.

□

5

Who will guard the guards themselves: The crime of omission

"There may be a hundred reasons to not do something and only one to do it- because it is the just thing to do."

The Doctrine of the Crime of Omission is to affix responsibility and accountability when a person mandated to complete a task or duty, does not do so.

A person charged with the protection of a right is even more guilty by omission, than the person committing the violation.

Any crime has two essential ingredients – *mens rea,* meaning intention, and *actus reus,* meaning action. Any act of crime may consist of commission, omission or possession. Omission here is a failure to act. The word "offence" while defining a crime in Indian law means "any act or omission made punishable by any law for the time being in force"[8].

*****

In December 2012, the fatal gang rape of a paramedical student in a moving bus in New Delhi triggered a nationwide call for stricter laws to ensure the safety of women. Public-spirited citizens, angry at the state of affairs, took to the streets. Thousands of students and eminent personalities were marched on to meet the President of India. My wife, Priyanka *ji,* nursing her fractured leg, cried watching these developments on television, all through Saturday, 22nd December 2012. She even wrote a pleading letter to the then Chief Justice of India (Justice Altamas Kabir) and kept urging me to go and join the protesters.

In the past, I had assisted various government agencies in the drafting of various policies for the protection of women and children. In my experience, the government agencies always wanted these policies to be drafted 'yesterday', meaning that there was always an urgency that was required on such occasions.

I wanted to go but instinctively knew that after so much of public outcry, the government was bound to do something. I did not know what was going to happen

8. (Section 2 (1)(q) of The Bharatiya Nagarik Suraksha Sanhita, 2023 (BNSS) the new criminal procedure code)

but knew that if I was needed to assist the government, I could not be out on the streets, and not in front of my computer.

On 23rd December, 2012, the government formed a Committee chaired by retired Chief Justice of India, Justice J. S. Verma. Justice Leila Seth, former judge of Delhi High Court, and Mr. Gopal Subramanium, former Solicitor General of India, were also on the Committee tasked with suggesting changes in the criminal law to provide for a swift trial and enhanced punishments in cases of sexual assault of an extreme nature.

A few days later, I had the misfortune of being called to depose before the Committee – misfortune because such a crime should never have taken place and such a committee should never have been formed.

But it was as such.

I was given 10 minutes to explain to the Committee the issue of missing children in India.

Post my submissions, I was about to leave after thanking the Committee member Mr. Subramanium, when I casually remarked, "I hope this Committee is looking at zero to rape, and rape and beyond".

"What do you mean by this?" he asked.

"There are multiple crimes that happen and go unpunished or unnoticed before a person becomes a rapist. These crimes are at home or are in commercial settings in the form of trafficking. A majority of victims do not come forward. And the small numbers that do, continue to remain on trial by the society and the justice delivery mechanisms. Each rape case is a trial of the economic pressures, social and mental resilience, patience, will and tenacity of the victim and her family," I said.

I had worked with Mr. Subramanium earlier in another BBA case before the Supreme Court when he was the Solicitor General of India in 2010. Trafficking had been defined in that case on 18th April, 2011, for the first time in India as per the United Nations definition, and India subsequently ratified the Palermo Protocol against Trafficking as a result of that judgement in May 2011.

A majority of institutional frameworks for child protection across India, like the child welfare committees, the Juvenile Justice Boards, regulation of child care institutions, and others had been established as a result of that judgement.

On that fateful day of my deposition before the Committee, Mr. Subramanium asked me to stay back and elaborate. He is extremely soft-spoken but one of the most eloquent individuals with an exceptional command over both Hindi and English languages, and is capable of quoting the ancient scriptures just as easily as he would precedents of law. And that day, he was both incisive and patient.

For the next five hours, I was in his office discussing crimes of varied nature against women in detail and left his office a little after 11pm. I was happy with what I had explained to the Committee, but came home apologetically as I had been assuring Priyanka *ji* every hour since 6:30 pm that I would be returning in another 30 minutes.

The following evening, to make amends, I decided to take Priyanka *ji* out for a street food festival. At about 8:30 pm, as soon as we sat down to eat, I received a call from Mr. Subramanium asking my whereabouts.

"Sir, I am having dinner," I said.

"The country is on fire, and you're having dinner? Why aren't you here?" he sounded irked.

I apologised saying I was not aware that I was supposed to join him that evening. He retorted, "Shame on you! Looking for an invitation."

I smiled at his forceful command with a right and sense of humour in those times. Since I was in the vicinity, I immediately apologised to Priyanka *ji,* leaving her to finish dinner, and left for Mr. Subramanium's office in Jor Bagh.

Over the course of the following weeks, I would go to his office every evening, work till the wee hours of the morning, come home to sleep for 3 – 4 hours, attend office in the morning to research and prepare for the evening again.

On the first night, I had dinner on my way back home at a 24x7 restaurant at Nizamuddin railway station. The next day, I went to a pizza place in Meher Chand Market near Jor Bagh and made a pact with a staff that I would give him money daily for leaving a pizza for me outside his outlet as his last order, that I could collect around 2 – 3 a.m. when returning home.

The second night I was happy, thinking I did not to have to worry about midnight dinner, only to discover a dog savouring the pizza. So on the third night, I asked the pizza person to tie the pizza up and hang it on the shutter of his store, away from the dogs. That became the norm for the following nights.

While dinner was invariably prepared at home, my love for pizzas meant that every night of work became an excuse for a pizza party. Those may not be the most delicious pizzas I have had, but as time would prove, they were certainly the most fulfilling and rewarding ones.

My main contention before the Verma Committee was that no one becomes a rapist overnight. A person starts with lesser crimes of a sexual nature and continues doing these small crimes over time. When these go unreported and unpunished, the impunity leads to heinous crimes like rape and gang rape.

I also discussed why different sexual crimes were not considered within the purview of law.

During one of those deliberations, I remembered something connected.

*****

While studying in Sri Venkateshwara college in South Delhi, in 1996, I met a girl who was being continuously stalked and harassed by one boy from her neighbourhood.

One day he came to college and started harassing her. The girl asked me for help as she was sitting next to me in the college lobby. I stopped him and got into a fight. A few days later, I again saw her at the college festival, this time walking arm in arm with that same boy. He came close to me and mouthed obscenities about the girl in front of her. I turned and walked away.

A few minutes later, she came back in a hurry, visibly scared and apologised to me. When I asked her what was the apology for, she replied for being in company of that boy. I told her there was no need to apologise. I would have done the same if she, or any other girl, was to ask for my help and at the end of the day it was her personal life and choice.

She replied pensively that it was not her choice. She had to go back to the same neighbourhood every evening and was scared of stepping out of her house at any time. If there was any scandal, her parents would stop her education and get her married off.

A teacher at school had once told me, "Man is born free but everywhere he is in chains." What could be a heavier chain than this? This girl did not have the support of her family, the support of her neighbourhood or society and did not have the support of law as what this boy was doing was neither illegal nor punishable in 1997.

This lack of any alternative course of action; this deprivation of choice, this compulsion of a girl to endure being continuously abused by her stalker if she wants to continue her education. This lack of freedom and equality, is the biggest evil, the biggest force being faced by a majority of girls and women in India.

Freedom from fear should be one of the main goals of a just society and any factor that deprives a person of the choice of alternatives creates a force that perpetuates this fear.

On the contrary, a force that ensures that a person does not infringe on the rights and space of another, a compulsion to stay on the course of law and order, and follow the path of being just, adds to the deterrence which is a force multiplier on the pathways of justice.

Fear should be in the mind of the perpetrator of a crime or a wrong and not in the mind of the victim. The fear has to be of law, reflective of the collective will and might of society. Thus, for a perpetrator, there needs to be a fear of committing crime and a fear of the retribution.

In 1996, I was 17. After this incident, whenever I went to the college, scenes of the fight with the boy and the girl's subsequent submission would haunt me everywhere. This incident left an indelible impression on me.

While I did not even know her name, within a week of this incident I dropped out of college, only to continue my graduation later through correspondence.

Years later, while practicing law and being faced with such similar situations with other friends and colleagues at the workplace, I realised that in India, the only crime of a sexual nature in such circumstances, was that of criminal assault with an intent to outrage the modesty of a woman, apart from rape. So anything which was less than forcible sexual intercourse was covered under Section 354 or Section 509 of the IPC, and stalking and sexual harassment were not explicitly defined as criminal acts.

As these acts were not considered a crime till 2013, even considered 'manly' at times, they were further glamourized and romanticized in movies and garnered societal acceptance. This only increased the impunity in sexual crimes as there was no fear of retribution.

Further, any action under these sections had to prove the existence of multiple elements of 'criminal assault' as well as an 'intent to outrage the modesty of a woman'.

There were reported cases of child sexual abuse where lawyers defending the accused had argued that an act of insertion of a finger in the vagina of a seven-month-old baby was not covered under any law. It was not an act of 'rape', not covered under Section 354 of IPC as a 6-month-old baby had no concept of 'modesty'. These preposterous arguments have been a part of legal discussions and even judgements.

While the law has evolved considerably and such arguments have now been settled, yet, in the absence of laws, these sexual acts were not recognised as crimes and had resulted in impunity for years.

*****

Back to the discussions with the Verma Committee.

The first challenge was to identify and propose the creation of multiple sexual crimes being faced by women and children in India that were not a part of law. These included sexual harassment, stalking, voyeurism, criminal assault to disrobe a woman, acid attack, etc., that were (and are) rampant in society.

The other issue requiring urgent intervention was,

as per me, the 'commercial or paid rape' of a child victim of trafficking. In 2004, a comprehensive study by the Ministry of Women and Child Development, Government of India, estimated that there were 2.8 million women in prostitution in the country, of which 36 per cent were children.

This meant that, even as per government estimates, about one million children were being subjected to 'paid rape' every day. If one was to assume even five sexual encounters with a child per day, the number of rapes or other sexual offences against children was a mindboggling five million according to 2004 data.

Five million rapes of children in a day as a result of having been trafficked, an act prohibited in the Constitution as a Fundamental Right under Article 23, that we, as a nation, were not even talking about. While the numbers would have certainly reduced since then, this paid rape continues even today.

The other form of invisible rape as a result of trafficking was through the placement agencies providing domestic labour for India's growing middle class. These agencies traffic girls from remote areas of Chhattisgarh, West Bengal, Odisha, Jharkhand, Assam and other states, use rape as a form of subjugation and control over these children.

While this is the worst form of slavery and sexual exploitation, it continues unabated in our homes and because of the demand created by us for cheap labour.

In fact, the only victim of sexual abuse that the Justice Verma Committee interacted with, was a child victim of trafficking for domestic labour, who had been subjected to blackmail, abuse and rape. Appalled at the state of affairs in the case, Mr. Subramanium, on behalf of the Committee even gave the child the wages that were due to her as reparation on behalf of the society so that she could move on and restart her life immediately.

The third issue was of missing children and especially in the context of trafficking, and the possible crimes they fall prey to.

The fourth was the ignominy of the epidemic of child sexual abuse in the country. Also, the need to incorporate the provisions of the (newly enacted) Protection of Children from Sexual Offences (POCSO) Act into the erstwhile Indian Penal Code and bring both laws in sync.

The fifth issue was that of marital rape and child marriage, both entrenched in our society even today.

The sixth issue was about the response of the State machinery to crimes of a sexual nature. Police accountability, the urgent need for victim-friendly procedures in Courts, time-bound trials, rehabilitation and compensation for the victims were discussed and deliberated upon in detail.

We worked on the language, contents and the punishments for each one of the proposed offences as well as creating an ecosystem for safety and protection of women.

Agreeing with our suggestions, the Committee recommended inclusion of new offences like trafficking, stalking, voyeurism, and affixing accountability of public servants, amongst others. The Justice Verma Committee Report went on to become one of the most holistic documents on prevention, protection and prosecution of sexual crimes against women and children and to further gender justice, in India. And in record time. The Report had been prepared and submitted within a month (23rd January 2013) of the formulation of the Committee; this meant that the government also had to act fast to assuage the public fury.

Within ten days, on 3rd February 2013, the Criminal Law Amendment Ordinance, 2013, was promulgated and notification issued. All our suggestions were now a part of law and trafficking was an explicitly defined crime in the Indian Penal Code (IPC) as Section 370 and Section 370 A, with the strictest possible punishments. My dream had come true. Or so I thought.

*****

I came to the office on the morning of Monday on 4th February, and as we celebrated our success, I announced to my colleagues my plans to retire and maybe pursue teaching. The next ten days were quiet and mostly spent in trying to comprehend the enormity of the previous month.

Destiny meanwhile smiled at the naivety of my plans. On the night of 13th February, Priyanka *ji* and I boarded the Habibganj – Nizamuddin Express at the Nizamuddin Railway station, along with my friend and colleague Vinay Singh, affectionately called Lanu *ji*. We were going to attend the wedding of my cousin in Vidisha, Madhya Pradesh. Before the train started, I received a phone call from the concerned officers in the Ministry of Home Affairs (MHA). They had some questions on the inclusion of crime of trafficking in the Ordinance that needed clarity that very night.

Fearing that they might want to tone down the strict punishments prescribed in the law, I asked Priyanka *ji* to continue on to Vidisha along with Lanu *ji* but without me.

After leaving her at around 8. 30 pm, as I was preparing to disembark from the train, it moved and in the push and pull of the last-minute passengers, I fell from the moving train. The excruciating pain from both my knees made me lose perception and for a minute I thought I was unconscious.

Gathering my wits and senses after a couple of minutes, I found my phone which had fallen apart in the melee. I called back the driver who had dropped us at the station, and asked the porters to help me get up and assist me in walking till the car. Once out and in the car, I went to a diagnostic centre at K. G. Marg where I was told that I had torn ligaments in both my knees and needed a plaster. There was no time to put on the plaster and rest. I tied my legs tightly with bandages and at about 9.45 pm, I reached the MHA.

The situation was worse than my worst fears. There was opposition to the very inclusion of trafficking in the IPC. Certain people within the government and the civil society believed that trafficking was not a sexual offence and felt that the Verma Committee had exceeded its brief by recommending its inclusion, especially the words 'forced labour' and 'prostitution' within its ambit and prescribing punishments up to life imprisonment for it.

We worked till late at night with data and arguments on why these amendments were needed in the law.

The next day, the Ordinance was referred to the Standing Committee of Home Affairs of the Parliament. Now, it was their decision to recommend how and what sections they wanted included in the final law.

The Standing Committee was a 30-member committee of parliamentarians headed by Mr. Venkaiah Naidu and had stalwarts such as Mr. L. K. Advani and Mr. D. Raja on it.

Each of them had to be now convinced on why these changes in law and the strict punishments had been proposed. The battle was not over yet.

The knees were slowly giving up and there was no way that we were going to lose this opportunity over stupid ligaments, I thought to myself. As I would walk slowly on crutches, with my legs firmly tied with bandages, meeting every single member of the Standing Committee over the course of the next few weeks, I realised how precarious the situation was. Many would call me over multiple times and discuss the data and laws in detail.

Some, like Mr. Raja, were compassionate and considerate for my condition and would come down to meet me at the under-renovation Constitution Club, so I would not have to walk all the way to his government-allotted flat on the third floor at Vitthalbhai Patel House.

In March, on the morning that the Standing Committee was supposed to make its final recommendations, the white chart paper on my wall said out of 30 members, 14 were positive and in favour of the law as it was, 15 were undecided and one was against the inclusion of strict laws against trafficking. In politics, being undecided mostly means 'no', but we had not lost all hope yet.

All the laws we had proposed were included, as was trafficking. The punishments were not reduced but the words 'forced labour' and 'prostitution' were expunged. Instead, 'physical exploitation' was included as a form of exploitation.

The Constitution of India had prohibited 'forced labour' as a 'form of traffic in human beings' under Article 23 and, along with untouchability, it is one of the only two constitutionally guaranteed Fundamental Rights that prescribe punishment. Yet, 'trafficking for forced labour' is still not a part of substantive law as a crime.

*****

The legal process, especially in cases of crime, works simultaneously on three fronts–

(A) Reparation for the victim

(B) Reformation and punishment for the guilty in such a way that there is no remission or repetition of the crime, and

(C) Deterrence in and for society.

The process of reparation for the victim of a crime, should aspire to, as far as possible, return the victim back to a similar situation that existed before the crime. This includes rehabilitation, compensation, protection as a victim/ witness and various other provisions that are made by the State from time to time.

Any omission in these processes, in a way, contributes to the non-delivery of justice, or the continuation of injustice.

The process of providing or securing rights is, in fact, like a jigsaw puzzle where each piece has an integral and important part to complete the picture and there is an interdependence of each piece on the other. In cases where right to justice is denied, each missing or broken piece leaves the entire picture incomplete.

In recent times, this evolving understanding that omission or denial of what is due to the victim is also an injustice, is increasingly being accepted as a crime itself.

For example, the newly introduced criminal law in India, The Bharatiya Nyaya Sanhita, 2023 (BNS), makes it mandatory for a public servant to register a case in instances of crimes, like rape or trafficking.

Similarly, all hospitals are mandated to provide treatment to victims of sexual offences and inform the police. In the BNS, and Protection of Children from Sexual Offences Act, 2012 (POCSO), mandatory reporting in many crimes has been introduced including sexual offences against children, which means that a failure to report a case of child sexual abuse is also a criminal offence.

This understanding is currently confined to the

reporting or registration of a crime, which is only the beginning of the legal process.

Denial of any of these rights must be made accountable and sanctions attached, as has been done in the case of non-registration of cases or non-treatment of victims. Thus, omission to provide what is due to a victim by duty-bearers should be treated as a crime in itself.

This is the Doctrine of Crime of Omission.

The accountability of public servants is seldom affixed. One of the most important shifts that was proposed by the Justice Verma Committee was on affixing accountability of public servants through the inclusion of a new section (Section 166A) which mandated that crimes of a sexual nature, such as sexual assault, rape, trafficking, etc. have to be compulsorily registered and investigated and a failure to do so by a public servant was a crime in itself. This was the purview of the crime of omission.

Many times, we, as a society, forget what already exists and what we have really done with what we have. The true mettle of a society is seen in how it responds to its own failures and accepts that a wrong to one is a wrong to all.

Either it can have "it is what it is" attitude, or it can respond with a will to identify the persons responsible and hold them accountable for their actions and omissions. Similarly, how a society incentivises good performance lays the motivation for action and responsibility.

In cases of omission, there is an inherent shifting of

blame or accountability between the society, the police and the judiciary.

The judiciary will find fault with the police, or the politicians, but there are hardly any cases where the judiciary has found fault within. The same is true for the police as well as the politicians.

Thus, all continue to remain in public service while the poor and uneducated continue to be subservient to a system of governance with little transparency and accountability.

While there is system of rating for the legislature through the democratically elected process, the same is not true for the executive and the judiciary. A fundamental shift where the performance of both the judiciary and the executive, including the police, is transparent and in the public domain, is one of the most critical missing pieces of the efficient performance of the legal system.

10 Years Later

"I feel that the constitution is workable, it is flexible and it is strong enough to hold the country together both in peacetime and in wartime. Indeed, if I may say so, if things go wrong under the new Constitution, the reason will not be that we had a bad Constitution. What we will have to say is that Man was vile."

—Dr. B.R. Ambedkar

In 2021, Khushi[9] a 13-year-old girl was allegedly gang raped by Mahender and Chandan in Lalitpur, Uttar

9. Name changed to protect identity

Pradesh. The very same day her mother went to the police station, but the police refused to register the FIR and the SHO[10] threatened her and sent her away.

On 14th November, as the country celebrated 'Children's Day', the SHO called the victim and her family to the police station and threatened them in the presence of one of the accused.

On 23rd November 2021, the victim's mother sent an application to the Superintendent of Police and filed an application before the concerned court for registration of an FIR, the very next day, i.e., 24th November.

A court order may not necessarily be justice but only an interpretation of facts and law which limits the citizens' rights to being a passive recipient of what the court (State) considers appropriate. And, that is the biggest disenfranchisement for a victim.

The court called her back again and again. No case was registered over the next five months, as the court listed the matter 11 times for hearing. As the victim was set to depose before the court and record her statement on 25th April 2022, she was kidnapped on 22nd April and again allegedly gang raped by Mahender and Chandan along with two others.

Her mother filed a missing child's complaint on 23rd April and even sent a complaint to the National Commission for Women about the missing child on 24th April 2022. She was given a complaint receipt number – 201411118227.

---

10. SHO or Station House Officer is the head or individual in charge of the locality police station

Her alleged kidnappers and rapists dropped her back near the police station in the wee hours of 26th April 2022. She waited from 5 am that day till the night of 27th April at the police station.

As the entire police station of over 20 policemen watched, the SHO Tilak Dhari, took Khushi to a room at the back and allegedly raped her. Then he sent her away with a woman to be taken to another village.

On 30th April 2022, a Sub-Inspector of Police called the local Childline (the Govt. helpline for children in need of care and protection) and asked them to take the girl away as she needed care and did not want to go back to her family. As she was with the Childline team, and received counselling, she narrated her ordeal. On Childline's intervention and their raising the issue before senior police officer, an FIR was finally registered on 3rd May 2022.

Later, upon my intervention, the Supreme Court of India took up this case. In December, 2023, the Court ordered that a support person should be appointed in every case of child sexual abuse to ensure that parents get assistance to navigate the legal process and the child as well as the family get mental health support. This is similar to the Supreme Court order on 10th May 2013 that a para-legal volunteer must be present in a police station to assist in cases of all crimes against children.

The law is enough, the policies exist. How they are read, implemented and how much are they implemented, and what parts are not implemented and what happens thereafter are the real tests of the system. The society needs to seek accountability of the people it has appointed to guard itself.

Systemic injustice is the outcome of omissions by duty bearers. A shift in how crimes are perceived in society at large, and towards robust institutional practices can help in preventing such omissions.

The policeman who allegedly raped the child was arrested and prosecuted. However, no action has been taken against all the other duty bearers that Khushi approached and who failed her. They continue without being held answerable.

Khushi was shifted from her home town to another state to continue for her education with support of an NGO. Her case is a prime example of the system's apathy- from the police to the courts to the national commission- for months the guards responsible for protecting her and acting on her complaint did not.

It is time to call these acts of omission at every stage in the delivery of justice, this apathy, for what it really is: A crime.

□

6

When a crime continues to live on: The continuity or perpetuity of crime

"Every person in a courtroom is earning from the delay in trials, apart from the victims and the society."

Crime continues to live on with the legal process.

Delays in the completion of legal process need to be made accountable as a crime itself.

In the absence of a swift and just response, the victim continues to pay for their loss, first through the crime itself, then through the loss of time, effort and dignity in the course of a prolonged legal process.

Usually, when a crime is committed, it is treated as a single crime and a punishment is prescribed in law. However, we have now enacted laws that mandate that in a situation where there is a continuation of a wrong, either through an act or through an omission, then such continuity of a wrong (crime) is not a single crime; rather it is to be treated as separate crimes, sometimes of a perpetual nature.

There exists such a precedent in the Juvenile Justice (Care and Protection of Children) Act, 2015 (JJ Act), that every month of delay in registration of a child care institution will be treated as a separate crime. If there is such a law for the citizens, similarly laws and policies prescribing an accountability framework for the State machinery responsible for the delays, at every stage of the legal and rehabilitation process, can also be made.

While this is a good provision in the law which has clearly worked effectively and has raised a precedent to be formulated along similar lines it raises another question. This is a law made by the State for the performance of an act, and omission, and subsequent delays have been criminalized. Thus, the very same principles may be extended to State bodies responsible for the delivery of rights.

This is the Doctrine of Continuity or Perpetuity of Crime.

*****

A quick look at the latest data from National Crime Records Bureau's (NCRB), Crime in India Report from

2022, gives a lot of answers and makes us ask some very difficult but pertinent questions.

The number of pending trials under POCSO Act in our courts stands at a staggering 243,237, as of 31st January 2023, with only 28,850 cases disposed of in 2022.

It will take not less than nine years to clear this backlog even if no new cases are added. Out of 268,038 cases that were in trial under the POCSO Act in 2022, only 8,909 cases, a paltry three per cent of the total number, resulted in convictions, and 18,202 cases resulted in an acquittal.

Even this three per cent is not the end of the legal process, as no specific data for cases under POCSO Act is available for pending appeals in higher courts. This horrifying current status is despite there being a law, which prescribes time-bound completion of trials within two months for rape and within one year for all other child sexual offences.

These stark numbers represent the long walk to justice for children and their families. They are also a small drop in the ocean of unreported cases, with research showing up to one in four children in India getting sexually harassed or abused. This points towards a grim situation where a large number of people are not reporting the crimes against them, perhaps due to a loss of faith in the justice delivery mechanisms, or a fear of the legal processes. We are, therefore, miles away from the idea of justice.

These numbers are astonishing for a robust law armed with seemingly adequate infrastructure and resources. Since 2019, over Rs. 1,900 crore[11] was allocated for 2023-2025 and over Rs. 1,000 crore has already been spent for the activation of fast track special courts (FTSCs) and infrastructure to complete the trial of POCSO cases.

On average, each of these courts have disposed off a mere 28 cases in the year 2022. The total budgetary spend on these FTSCs was Rs. 786.43 crores. Thus, on an average the outcome of these FTSCs was that each disposed off case ended up costing the state about Rs. 273,000.

Although the actual indicator of success is the total number of disposed off cases with respect to the total amount of money spent, but if we were to consider only convictions as the benchmark for the success of the FTSCs, then 8,909 convictions in POCSO cases came after spending Rs. 880,000.

This budgetary allocation, as a part of a special scheme, was introduced in September 2019 to clear the pendency and the backlog. However, both have only increased since. The following examples indicate the gravity of the situation and the time it will take for the states to clear the backlog of POCSO cases, provided no new cases are added-

- Arunachal Pradesh will take 35 years;
- Delhi will take 27 years;
- Bihar will take 26 years;
- West Bengal -will take 25 years; and so on

11. One Crore is equal to 10 million

The trial process is but a small part in the overall justice framework in the translation of our laws into justice. The time frame of investigation and trial are both prescribed in the laws. Yet, even this small part has not been ensured.

It is anything, but just, for a society to have a child be raped and forced to continue to wait for justice in courts till she is a mother, or even a grandmother.

*****

"When a child is bought or sold, the purpose is immaterial."

Usman *ji*, an office assistant at BBA, vehemently argued in the middle of a packed conference room in early July, 2014.

Mostly uneducated, and known for his upfront attitude, Usman *ji* is a short man with a moustache and a smiling and disarming demeanour, who kick-starts our work day with his morning tea laced with his love and warmth. In the last 25 years, BBA has grown with Usman *ji*.

The death of Nirbhaya was a pivotal moment in India's understanding and response mechanisms against sexual crimes. The brutality in the death of the departed soul scarred a generation for life, but paved the way for the protection of generations hence, through amendments in various laws.

I was sitting with the entire BBA team, deliberating on recommendations for a proposed amendment to the JJ Act. The government wanted to reduce the age of culpability in heinous offences, from 18 years to 16 years, as one of the accused in the murder was a juvenile and had been released after spending three years in an observation home.

We were discussing what we wanted incorporated in the proposed Act. The three major areas of our recommendations were; the inclusion of checks and

balances in crimes committed by children between the ages of 16 to 18 years; strengthening of the institutional frameworks for rehabilitation and adoption, including registration of children's homes; emerging crimes against children like use of a child by an adult to commit a crime, attempt to marry a child, and trafficking, amongst others.

As we discussed the gaps in the protection of children from trafficking, since the law required a purpose of trafficking to be established, Usman *ji* contended that buying or selling of a child itself is a crime. Why should one have to prove the purpose of it? We were surprised at his clarity and simplicity. He may not have received a formal education, but his common sense of justice was more formidable than the existing laws on trafficking.

We suggested this in the draft and it was subsequently accepted, before becoming a part of the law as section 81 of the JJ Act.

Another major inclusion in the law was a specific provision that required every child care institution or children's home to be registered within six months of the law being enacted. It also mandated that in case a child care institution did not register, it could be fined at least Rs. 100,000 and the person–in–charge could be imprisoned for a period up to one year.

The most important and path breaking provision of this Section 43 of the JJ Act was that in cases of such non-registration, a delay of every 30 days would be considered a separate offence.

This meant that a person (herein the person-in-charge of the child care institution) would face a fine of

Rs. 1,200,000 if he did not register in time for a year, or even Rs. 12,000,000 if he did not register for ten years.

After the enactment of this law, the Child Care Institutions registered themselves, and the number of registered institutions increased from 1,757 in 2014[12] to 7,109 in 2018[13].

So the law worked.

*****

As discussed earlier, several laws were amended after the Nirbhaya case and came into effect on 3rd February 2013.

Yet a few months later, in April 2013, when five-year-old girl Gudiya (Hindi for 'doll') was kidnapped and brutally raped in northeast Delhi's Gandhinagar area, the police did little apart from registration of an FIR. Two days later, she was found locked up in a room in the same building where she lived, by a neighbour in the wee hours of the morning when he overheard a child's weak wails from the locked room.

When Gudiya was found, it was no less than a miracle that she was still alive. She was found bleeding and unconscious for almost 36 hours with grievous injuries and foreign objects inside her. When the child was taken to the hospital, Gudiya's father who was a vegetable vendor alleged that the police had promised to give him Rs. 2,000 with an assurance that the child would be taken care of medically, if he hushed up the matter. The father refused and created a furore.

12. Lok Sabha, unstarred question 1416, dated 18th July 2014
13. Lok Sabha, unstarred question 1678, dated 20th July 2018

Journalists too raised the issue and within a few days, BBA moved an application before the Supreme Court of India demanding that the police needed to do more than merely registering of the FIR.

The law on missing children was laid down, a standard operating procedure (SOP) for cases of missing children was created and thousands of missing children were saved over the next decade.

Gudiya was relocated, her education was continued in one of the best private schools and she was given exemplary compensation of Rs. 1,100,000 with some corporate bodies coming to her aid for medical assistance. However, her court case continued.

In March 2014, one of the two accused, Pradeep, pleaded juvenility and produced an old attendance register of his school as an official record to support his claim. As per law, a school attendance register is not a proof of age, but his plea was allowed nevertheless. He was declared a juvenile at the time of the crime, and released in April 2017.

As I went through the records, it was clear to me that his name was added subsequently in the attendance register, and most probably, it was a forged document.

Now that the accused had been released, the poor, uneducated parents of Gudiya were dependent on the willingness of the State machinery to act further.

Despite being one of the most high-profile incidents, the fate of the case rested upon the labyrinth nature of the legal process. The benefit of doubt goes to the accused, but in this case, the law was clear on the process of age determination. Yet, it was being wrongly interpreted in favour of the accused.

The Protection of Children from Sexual Offences Act, (POCSO) 2012, is clear that the burden of proof is on the accused. Still, the systemic leaning of the legal process towards protecting the rights of the accused, and not the rights of the victims, or the ends of justice was apparent here too and Pradeep had walked free.

Representing the victim, BBA approached Senior Advocate Mr. H. S. Phoolka, who agreed to file the appeal against the acquittal before the Delhi High Court. Mr. Phoolka is one of India's leading human rights lawyers and has been fighting for justice for victims of crime since 1984.

Bespectacled, with a white, neatly tucked beard, and looking much older than his real age, he is best known for representing thousands of victims killed in the Sikh genocide and riots in the aftermath of Prime Minister Indira Gandhi's assassination in 1984.

Like me, he had also started as a young lawyer, fighting for legal justice. I had first requested for his guidance in 2008 and in the very first case where he had represented BBA, trafficking had come to be defined, which led to the formation of the law later on.

Over time, he started representing and guiding BBA in all its legal cases *pro bono.* Despite charging no fee, his knowledge, intelligence and commitment brought about an incisiveness in child protection issues across the country. He has helped hundreds of thousands of children in need of care and protection through the court judgements that changed the entire ecosystem of child protection in India.

One of the biggest impediments in the advancement and growth of society is that the delivery of justice has become subservient to knowledge, power, money and the ability to hire lawyers who would continue the fight. In most cases, while the public prosecutors or legal-aid lawyers would give up after an adverse order or judgement, but lawyers engaged by the accused would continue to pursue the case because of its benefits. There are only a few lawyers like Mr. Phoolka, who devote their knowledge, skill, and acumen towards the ends of justice for the needy.

His approach that a good lawyer knows when to speak and a great lawyer knows when to shut up is a lesson to emulate for all budding legal practitioners.

Mr. Phoolka passionately argued that Pradeep's plea of juvenility was a complete farce and a reinvestigation was required. The Delhi High Court then directed the trial court to again conduct an enquiry into Pradeep's juvenility claims. As a result of this re-enquiry, the trial Court declared Pradeep was not a juvenile in March 2018.

Eventually, both the accused were convicted with 20 years of rigorous imprisonment, and as of 2024, their appeals are pending before the High Court of Delhi.

The seemingly never ending legal process, and this continuation of crime really boils down to the ends of justice being dependent upon the following – knowledge, resources, time or patience, and will.

The one with more of these four, invariably has an upper hand in most legal processes.

*****

I was talking to a gang rape victim a few years ago whose case had been going on for over three years. One of her alleged rapists had been released on bail by the High Court and had moved back to live in the same neighbourhood.

As she sat with me, crying and, narrating how her life had ended, I said to her, "Time heals all wounds."

She replied, "No it does not; it only lessens the pain.

And only sometimes; other times, it worsens the pain."

Her father sitting next to her had added, "I want to kill the people who did this to my daughter."

I sat there silently looking at the floor and questioning my own inability and ineffectualness to do more. I thought about my failure; our collective failure as a society. Can the system and the State not see that there is an increasing powerlessness and simmering anger in society? An anger where a poor, helpless father is left with no choice but to think about murdering his daughter's rapist as he cannot hope for much else from the system and the society that he is a part of.

For this girl, time had come to a standstill since the day she was assaulted. She believed that her life, as she knew it, had ended.

Her wait had not.

*****

Crime is an act of transgression against an individual that requires a response from the society. To protect their own rights, the citizens in a society create, and continuously pay for the upkeep of law and order, and ensure the functioning of legal frameworks and institutions through the payment of taxes.

Therefore, when a section of society, namely the citizenry, has already paid for certain rights and privileges and has entrusted another section of society, namely, the police, judiciary and other similar duty-bearers with the delivery of the same, then automatically, the duty-bearers are custodians of this responsibility.

These custodians are in the service of society for the society itself. They are catalysts and conduits for ensuring the delivery of rights and therefore, need to be held accountable if there is any snag or delay in the delivery of rights.

Delays in the legal process cost the society and the country in terms of economic costs and loss of morale. And therefore, the accountability of such delays needs to be affixed.

Moreover, the society is paying for these systems of governance to ensure an adequate and just response to the crime itself. In case, this response is not just, or is inadequate, or there is an inordinate delay in ensuring this response, the victim continues to be victimized, and there is no deterrence in society.

While clichés like "justice delayed is justice denied" are popular parlance, for the victim, this denial defeats the entire notion of justice delivery and the crime continues to exist.

Any act or omission which aids and abets in this continued existence of crime, especially for a victim, is revictimization.

This becomes a vicious circle – scars and revictimization continue for the victim, while the delay propagates a sense of impunity for the criminals and in the long run this seeds a sense of legitimization of the crime in the society.

*****

81,498 IS NOT JUST A NUMBER!

One of the biggest issues concerning the application of laws is the trust deficit between the various stake holders and duty bearers.

Currently, the average person is inherently hesitant in approaching the police. The general perception is that the police do not care, are inactive and ineffective. This results in a lack of trust.

Moreover, whenever there is an increase in the number of crimes, especially serious crime, it tends to raise a question among the general masses regarding the deteriorating law and order. This further creates a pressure on the police from within, and sometimes even from outside, to under-report and showcase a healthy report card of crime under control.

This under-reporting results in a situation where the crime is not registered as such and the legal process does not even start, thereby creating a vicious circle.

The average person by and large has immense respect for the judiciary, but little faith in the processes of justice delivery which are considered complicated, lengthy and cumbersome. In courts, they are completely dependent on the lawyers, because they lack even the basic understanding of the legal processes.

Moreover, the courtroom jargon is an alien world for most. This results in a feeling of disempowerment for the victims in the legal processes. Thus, people tend to shy away from even approaching the courts or seeking justice as they believe that they will be further victimised through the process, thus resulting in a majority of crimes not getting reported.

This is exacerbated with the police not trusting the average person because they believe that people (victims) often report crimes in anger and often change their statements before the judge during the trial, thus negating all the hard work and efforts of the police during investigation.

Judges, by virtue of their position, need to be mindful of police excesses, and their over-stepping of legal boundaries. The continued oversight and questioning approach by the judges automatically results in a trust deficit between the judiciary and the police.

More often than not, judges tend to blame shoddy investigations or mistakes in procedure for the resulting acquittals. Also they too do not trust the public, as victims often change their statements. There is a general feeling within the judiciary that victims often misuse the laws.

The abuse of the legal processes by the victims cannot be ruled out. However, enough checks and balances exist within the legal systems to prevent misuse which are also being seldom used by the Police and the judiciary to stop this abuse and create a deterrent against it.

The few times that people misuse the law to falsely accuse another, or change their statements after reaching a compromise with the accused, or in instances of any other such misuse, these checks and balances need to be used by the legal machinery to uphold the sanctity of the law. However, instead of punishing the guilty, here too these few instances are used to brush aside the larger issues of crime infestation and impunity of crime in the society.

Thus, lack of trust at all levels on the part of the victims, police and the judiciary are often the primary reasons for the larger failure of the legal system in preventing crimes through a process of retribution, reformation and deterrence.

*****

In 2016, in one of the cases filed by me, a question was raised before the bench of the Chief Justice of Delhi High Court as to why compensation was not being provided to victims of child sexual abuse despite a robust Victims' Compensation Policy.

The Chief Justice said that we would look at it as an administrative issue. A meeting of judges of POCSO courts was held, and it was suggested that the witnesses were changing their testimonies during the trial, and therefore, did not deserve compensation from the State.

There are two elements in the trial process - one is to establish the crime, and the other is to establish the guilt. In matters of sexual violence against women and children, the extraneous factors at play have a very important role in determining the guilt. The economic status of the victims, coupled with the delays, again create a vicious circle.

The judges decided not to award compensation to victims of child sexual abuse on the premise that if victims were to turn hostile during the trial, the compensation amount would go waste. What this resulted in was that victims would only be paid the compensation amount after conviction.

Victims are in no way responsible for the conviction, but again, this mistrust of the judges was putting the victims through the trial and not the accused, especially in a law where the burden of proving guilt is not on the State, and the burden of proving his innocence is on the accused.

On 19th January 2024, I was sitting with a group of parents of child sexual abuse victims whose cases were in court (under trial). The parents were mostly poor and as I spoke to them about their future plans for their children, I found that they had none.

I asked if they had received any support from the government or the courts, they replied in the negative. One parent got up from the group to say that he had received interim compensation. The rest of them had not received any compensation. All those children between the ages of five to 15 had also stopped going to school.

This raises a larger question – Is compensation a right of the individual where the crime has been committed or is it a subject of the benevolence of the State or in this case, the courts? What about cases where conviction is not given? Crime has taken place but not proved or the accused was not found?

A court judgment may not necessarily be justice but only an interpretation of facts and laws. This limits the citizens' rights to only being a passive recipient of what the court (State) considers appropriate.

In all these cases, children's names continued in schools while they had dropped out. Thanks to the efforts of some of my colleagues, within the next few days every child had returned back to school and was receiving psychological and mental health support.

But these were children who were lucky. In 2021, while hearing a bail application in a rape case, a single judge bench of Justice Manoj Ohri of the Delhi High Court, asked if the victim had received any compensation. Upon hearing that she had not, Justice Ohri expanded the scope of the bail matter to find out the number of cases of rape and child sexual abuse where compensation had been awarded.

Shockingly, it was found that in Delhi alone, during 2012-2017, compensation was not given in 87,405 cases of rape and child sexual abuse.

This was the situation in the capital on a matter where an entitlement was put in place and budgeted for by the government. The victim compensation scheme had been formulated to ensure that victims of crimes are compensated to ensure that they are supported through medical and other expenses and also as reparation for the crime against them. Still this compensation was not being awarded for years when this information was put before the Court.

Legal services authorities also admitted that while they were willing to act on this information, they did not have enough lawyers and resources. Thus, they would not be able to deal with such a large number of backlog in compensation cases.

Young and dynamic lawyers, Ms. Prabhsahay Kaur and Ms. Rachna Tyagi, decided to think and act outside the box, with a 'never say die' attitude and a will for justice. Appeals were put up on the notice boards of all the trial courts in Delhi, asking lawyers to volunteer or work for expenses. A number of public-spirited lawyers joined hands to support the cases and assisted the Legal Services Authority in about 5,916 out of the identified 8,816 cases found fit to receive compensation.

In the rest of the 81,498 cases, there is now no scope for compensation as either the victims are untraceable or there are no details available to whether compensation is awardable or not.

81,498 is not a number.

These are lives. Families. Women. Children. Who have a right guaranteed by law and paid for by society.

And they did not even know for years that this right existed. And when the child, or the victims do not know, and are revictimized during the process itself, this hopelessness and helplessness felt by the millions that languish in the courtrooms every single day, without knowing what lies ahead in store for them, is amongst the biggest losses both in terms of the economy as well as the morale of the nation.

Till Justice Ohri went above and beyond his call of duty to ensure justice, many 'others' in positions of decision making, whose offices and benefits are also paid for by the society, had decided that the right did not exist.

Closure for the victim, victim reparation as far as

possible, punishment for the accused and deterrence for the society to prevent crime is the essence of the legal process. Public has an ephemeral memory, and thus, if the crime and its punishment do not embed together as an associated memory, their take away is crime with impunity.

The victims remain on tenterhooks, and are further victimised and disempowered if a crime goes unpunished, or in cases where there may be a decade-long wait for compensation or for the legal process to complete.

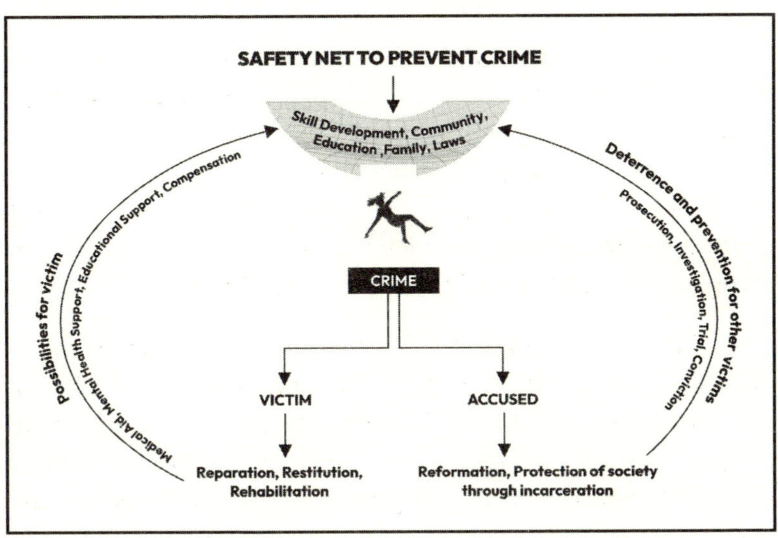

Till the time the case continues, whether in the lower courts or in the appeals process till the Supreme Court, the crime continues to exist in the mind of the victim who seeks closure in punishment for the guilty. As long as the victim is a part of the legal process, there is absence of this closure and the victim continues to suffer in all spheres, long after the crime was committed.

Consequently, the society too loses faith in the entire justice delivery system and the trust deficit between the public, the police and the judiciary is further widened. It is this apathy and lack of trust which means that while 50,000,000 people continue to be in courtrooms in the hope of justice[14], there are many more who are not even approaching the system to seek justice for the crime committed against them.

Many victims prefer to distance themselves from the legal process and attempt to move on, despite the trauma of the crime impacting them throughout life.

We need more judges like Justice Ohri; more lawyers like Mr. H.S. Phoolka, Ms. Prabhsahay Kaur and Ms. Rachna Tyagi. It is their actions that continue to ensure the application of law and expand the scope of justice to open the Pandora's box. But, even if these wrongs are corrected today, the time, the cost, the losses from the delays and the non-performance need to be accounted for.

Time is our greatest asset as well as our greatest liability. The time taken to register an FIR, for rehabilitation, or compensation, or victim protection, or victim witness relocation or medical or mental health assistance, or dispose of appeals in higher courts – all are a part of the legal processes of justice delivery.

Every stage of the legal process, especially where such a stage is time-bound as per law or policy, needs to be respected and the people responsible for administering and completing that stage, be held accountable. The delays at every stage should be compensated to the victim in accordance with the time taken.

---

14. Source: www.njdg.ecourts.gov.in

Victims from various socio–economic backgrounds such as poverty, lack of education, caste system, and other similar vulnerabilities, require continued assurance and assistance at every step of the legal process as, in most cases, they are not aware of any of their rights and entitlements.

The laws are increasingly being formulated with provisions that aim to ensure child or victim-friendly court procedures, fast track special courts, appointment of support persons to aid mental health and help in navigating the legal systems, and compensation, etc. Corresponding rules and schemes have also been framed that provide for budgetary allocations and institutional framework to implement these provisions. Access to these is, therefore, a right of the victims.

But all this remains largely on paper.

It is only just that if a delinquent child care institution can be fined Rs. 100,000 for each subsequent month of non-registration as a separate offence, then a judge can also be fined. At least the victim's compensation must be increased in proportion with the duration of the delay, and every person responsible for the same, held accountable.

*****

The law says that every case of rape reported to a police station needs to be registered, and failure to do so is itself a crime.

The law says that every victim of crime who has suffered loss or injury, and who required rehabilitation, is entitled to compensation.

The law says the trial in a rape case should be completed within two months as far as possible.

The laws say.

And the case continues.

□

7

No one gets left behind: The law must protect all

"When a child is before a judge, the society is on trial."

Every law must ensure that it is not only providing protection to every innocent, but it is also ensuring access to legal recourse to every victim.

In July 2023, while reading the morning newspaper, I came across a news that the Law Commission was almost ready with its report on the reduction of the 'age of consent' in India.

Till this time, I had actually not paid much attention to the entire debate around reducing the age of consent and amending the laws accordingly. I was presuming, albeit wrongly, that this clamour was more of an academic and research discourse and would gradually be countered with additional data and facts.

However, this was now serious. I immediately tried to set up a meeting with the Law Commission and fortunately, Mr. O. P. Singh, retired Director General of Police of Uttar Pradesh, and I were invited by the Chairperson of the Law Commission, Justice (retired) Mr. Ritu Raj Awasthi in the following week.

Mr. Singh was heading an organisation combatting online child sexual abuse and we had been working together for child protection for some time. He had known the chairperson during his previous assignments as well.

He had invited us at his home and had given a half an hour time slot for the meeting.

Before the meeting, I started researching the issue and history of this discussion. I discovered that in November 2022, a report was published to mark a decade of the Prevention of Children from Sexual Offences (POCSO) Act. The salient finding in the report, an analysis of judicial data, was that a majority of cases of sexual abuse were actually cases of elopement or romantic relationships.

The report was conducted in Assam, Maharashtra and West Bengal, and involved studying 7,478 special court judgements between 2016 and 2020. Of these, 7,064 cases came under POCSO Act and 1,715 were identified as 'romantic cases'.

In December 2022, delivering his keynote address at the National Annual Stakeholders Consultation on Child Protection, the Chief Justice of India, Hon'ble Mr. Justice D.Y. Chandrachud, said that cases of consenting minors being tried under POCSO Act posed difficult questions for judges across the spectrum and urged the legislature to look into this aspect in view of the 'reliable research'.

In the same year, various bodies of United Nations published a policy brief titled *Implication of the POCSO Act in India on Adolescent Sexuality* advocating that consensual sexual acts involving adolescents above 16 years of age should be decriminalised.

In the wake of these reports, there was an increasing clamour amongst the media, the judiciary and the civil society to reduce the age of consent under the POCSO Act on the premise that consensual sexual activity among adolescents was being criminalised under the law. Under POCSO Act, any sexual activity with a child under 18 years of age constitutes rape or penetrative sexual assault, with the consent being immaterial.

Several High Courts asked the Law Commission to look into this aspect and recommend reducing the age of consent under POCSO. This sent an erroneous message that most cases of child sexual abuse were cases of romantic relationships and media publicity around this assumption built up a hype that POCSO Act was a highly misused law, and innocent adolescents in love were only being victimised.

*****

As we reached the house of the Chairperson, we realised that it was, in fact, a camp office[15] and what we had presumed to be a brief meeting over tea was a full submission.

Suddenly, I felt underprepared as I was not carrying any documents, researches or any other data of any kind. There were several members of the commission present along with their full research team.

We were informed of the reference received from the Karnataka High Court and other courts regarding this matter. As the meeting continued, several issues came to be discussed and we were given an opportunity to speak freely.

I apologised to the commission saying that I may be permitted to speak from memory and allowed to make written submission later. I also sought forgiveness for any disparity in data of my oral and written submissions.

We tried to submit as much as we could from memory. Immediately thereafter, both Mr. Singh and I, sent our written submissions separately.

As the deliberations started, I realised that there were widespread misconceptions regarding how the laws were being misused and only one side of the story was being promoted loudly and vehemently.

We started by explaining to the commission that it must understand that it is not really deliberating on the

15. Camp Office is a temporary office operating from home

reduction of the 'age of consent under the POCSO Act', rather introducing it. As the law stands today, there is no concept of 'age of consent', so the issue of its reduction does not arise at all. It would be the introduction of a new concept, a new section that would have to be introduced in the law specifying 'consent' and 'age of consent'.

The Chairperson, Justice Awasthi explained that the main issue was the question raised before the commission regarding how POCSO Act was being misused and romantic relationships between adolescents were being criminalised. Children were also being put in jails on the complaint of parents in cases of non-acceptance by the family in romantic relationships, or in cases of elopement.

Elaborating on the misuse of the law, I explained that this was more the case of its misuse than an issue in the law, or legal process itself. When a child, especially a girl really elopes, she is considered missing and after the Supreme Court judgement of 2013, the case of the missing child is treated as a case of kidnapping or trafficking and is registered as such.

It is only after the girl is recovered and she gives a statement wherein there is an element of a crime of a sexual nature, can the police invoke the sections of the POCSO Act. It is also pertinent to understand that kidnapping or abduction for the purpose of illicit or sexual intercourse with a child are and have been offences under the law in the Indian Penal Code since 1860!

Therefore, the POCSO Act will only be used if and when the child alleges sexual abuse and this right should not be taken away from a child who is between 16-year-old to 18-year-old, especially in our country where a lot of external factors and influences play a part in the victims changing their statements and turning hostile.

It would be a travesty of justice if the law does not come to the aid of a family when a girl goes missing and the police, under the pretext of 'consent' or 'elopement', does not register the case. I reminded the commission of the situation in Nithari in 2006 and in the whole country prior to the Supreme Court judgement of 2013.

If we assume that it is indeed true and an element of consent is included in the law, or the age of consent is reduced through an amendment, will this amendment ensure that the POCSO Act is not misused?

Also, if both the victim and the accused are, in fact, in a romantic relationship, then the chances of them being in the similar age groups are very high. And under the Juvenile Justice (Care and Protection of Children) Act, 2015, no child is arrested and sent to prison.

While the system is full of checks and balances to protect any child who is accused of an offence under the POCSO Act, we need to focus all our energies on the protection of the child victims.

One of the other members raised further questions about the parents or children changing statements and informing the courts later on during the trials that they had indulged in sexual intercourse out of their own volition and the courts are constantly faced with this conundrum as so much of time, energy, effort and money is being wasted on these cases.

I strongly argued that we, as a society, can only accept the changed statements or testimonies of the children or parents when we ensure that their rights have been ascertained and provided for.

We are not completing investigations or trials within stipulated time; we are not paying compensation due to the victims; nor are we ensuring their protection, rehabilitation and education. Under these circumstances, how do we ascertain if the statements have not been amended under coercion, duress, or a frustration with an indifferent and insensitive system?

Sharing my personal experiences in cases, I spoke about a case in 2023 before the Delhi High Court. A child was allegedly gang raped by four people. She had filed the complaint before the police, given statement before a magistrate, deposed before a trial court judge in May 2023.

She had appeared in person, before the Delhi High Court in early July2023, as the bail application of the main accused was being heard. She informed the court that she had no objection to the bail being granted and that she did not even recognize the lawyer who was fighting her case.

I recounted cases and instances of courts asking rape victims to marry their rapists.

A man booked under the POCSO for rape was granted bail by the Allahabad High Court on the condition that he will marry the victim and will accept her child (born out of the alleged rape) as daughter.[16]

---

16. https://www.thehindu.com/news/national/other-states/allahabad-hc-grants-bail-to-pocso-accused-on-condition-that-he-marries-victim/article66010003.ece

Or a case in 2015, wherein a rapist was granted bail to meet his victim who was raped at the age of 15 and had a child as a result of the assault, with the court insinuating a 'happy outcome' – hinting at the possible marriage between the rapist and his victim and even citing alternative dispute resolution mechanisms.[17]

These cases, in my opinion, are a mockery of laws and a complete denial of the right to live with personal liberty and dignity for the victim child, which is her right under the Constitution of India.

Another example was of a case in which Odisha High Court had quashed an FIR against a 35-year-old married man with four children, accused of raping a 16-year-old child citing her 'consent' in a 'romantic relationship'. Paedophiles were preying on our young children in the name of romantic relationships in the era of digital connectivity.

*****

The society had failed these children when a crime against them could not be prevented. The society continued its failure in not being able to rehabilitate them. And now, the society had failed these children again in the delivery of justice, continuing their revictimization.

Moreover, the role played by external factors also needs to be taken into consideration. The social stigma and ostracization faced by the child and family, media glare, lack of protection from the accused, denied interim compensation or relief, increased vulnerabilities in cases

17. https://www.ndtv.com/chennai-news/rapist-victim-should-get-together-tamil-nadu-womens-panel-chiefs-shocker-775338

of incest or where the accused is known, lack of medical and psychological assistance, delays in the legal process and other similar factors, each play a part.

Despite the delays in trial and compensation, the children manage to overcome the trauma with the help of their families or others and do not wish to go through the trial process that is a reminder of the heinous crime. In such situations also, the children turn hostile as they want to escape the memories and continued trauma during the prolongation of the trial.

Therefore, the courts need to probe the various reasons given above and find out why the child turns hostile, instead of taking their changed statements at face value and believing them outright.

Moreover, the children and the families are under tremendous pressure in many child marriage or trafficking situations. This is more true where children become victims of Stockholm syndrome, identifying and empathizing with their perpetrators. For example, in situations of trafficking and online child sexual abuse, children are often groomed to think that it is in their best interest to continue to be exploited.

This is where the society needs to step in and ensure that the rule of law provides protection to all. What a child believes may not necessarily be in his or her best interest.

In India, as per a government response to a question in the Parliament in 2014, at least 1,200,000 children were in prostitution and other forms of commercial sexual exploitation. This 'paid rape' has implicit consent due to the transactional nature of the payment of money for raping (sexually abusing) a child whose consent is immaterial, by virtue of being a child as well as having been trafficked.

When it is already an established fact that a majority of girls are trafficked for sexual purposes, the inclusion of 'consent' in the POCSO Act may also be used as a tool by traffickers during the trial and would invariably lead to cross-examination of a victim, and making the entire trial process central to the conduct of the victim rather than that of the accused.

Moreover, there is a lack of robust laws to tackle emerging forms of sexual abuse and exploitation where consent maybe deemed as implicit, such as online grooming, sexual conduct through video games, and online child sexual abuse material.

*****

Before the Commission, I recounted an incident.

In April 2023, while addressing leaders from 161 NGOs that work for supporting victims and ensuring access to justice in over 10,000 child sexual abuse cases across India, I had asked them about the status of implementation of rehabilitation and compensation frameworks by courts.

They shared that in most cases, courts refused to entertain compensation applications citing 'romantic relationships', especially in cases where the victim was above 12 years. The courts were openly saying that compensation would only be paid after the conviction as victims change statements after receiving compensation.

I asked the Commission if the legal process could become vindictive. If a few individuals were changing their statements before courts and turning hostile despite receiving compensation, can this arguments be used to deny compensation to all other victims?

Is it not better to pay compensation to a hundred underserving people than to not pay to the one deserving person who would have faced hardships on account of a vengeful system? Is it not an act of revenge and punishment being meted to everyone on account of the wrongs of a few? Are we not going against the very notion of 'innocent until proven guilty'?

I implored with the Commission to consider all these factors and circumstances, as they have been completely negated or not considered in the debate to reduce the age of consent.

The media's one-sided approach and coverage also played a part in influencing people holding responsible positions. Without understanding the implications of what such an amendment in law might mean for the most vulnerable, the poorest of the poor children, various courts and judges also took this position.

All children must be protected under law, and similarly no innocent child should suffer. Therefore, I recommended a system of checks and balances.

The courts should have the discretion to look at genuine cases wherein the minimum punishment under

POCSO can be reduced or completely done away with, in certain situations.

These maybe where the victim is over 16 years of age, where the age difference between the two individuals is less than three years, where the accused has no past criminal history, there is no element of trafficking or undue influence, or coercion, or violence, where the victim has been steadfast in her/ his statements, etc.

While such a cautious and nuanced approach would protect young couples in genuine romantic relationships, it would also ensure that no child is left unsafe and without legal protection.

*****

"Innocent until proven guilty."

"Let a 100 guilty be acquitted but one innocent should not be convicted."

These two, amongst the most popular theories in jurisprudence, lay the foundation for the application of the rule of law in society.

However, to be able to move beyond the rule of law towards a rule of justness, the legal system needs to look beneath the surface and beyond these two maxims.

Both these are tilted towards the protection of legal rights of the accused. Over time, their continued application has led to the entire legal system being obsessed with the fact that no innocent should be ever punished.

Thus, the balance of scale is heavily tilted toward

the rights of the accused. The rights of the victims also require due consideration in parity with the rights of the accused.

The biggest challenge for any legal system is to find a balance between any misuse of law and ascertaining the guilt and surety of conviction for a crime.

In most criminal acts, the crime is against the society and the burden of proof for proving guilt is also on the society. Thus, every criminal case is referred to as State vs ABC. However, even in crimes like child sexual abuse, where the burden of proof is not on the state but has been shifted to the accused, the criminal trials are generally conducted in the same manner of ascertaining guilt due to the conditioning and the mind-set of the entire legal system – from police to public prosecutors to the judiciary.

Therefore, somehow, even in these cases, the burden of proof for proving guilt, is transferred vicariously from the State onto the victim. And in most cases, for all practical purposes, it is the victims who have to prove that what they are saying is the truth, with little help from the State.

Similarly, in policy formulation, there is tremendous pressure to adhere to the above-mentioned maxims. What this results in is that laws are formulated with an aim to protect every innocent, and not to ensure protection to every victim, or with an aim to ascertain responsibility in each and every circumstance.

Almost a Year Later

In September 2023, after examining the issue in great detail, the Law Commission made a clear-cut recommendation against reducing the 'age of consent'.

The Commission also accepted all my suggestions and recommended provisions for amendments in the POCSO Act accordingly.

The law must protect the innocent, both from being falsely accused or convicted, and from being a victim of a crime.

No one should get left behind in the pursuit of justice on account of the law not being present.

One wrong or one crime left unaccounted for, even one victim who cannot and will not get justice due to a lack of legal protection being available, is one too many.

If the law fails to protect one, it fails to protect all.

□

8

Don't look away: Societal acceptance is promotion of crime

"Because it is needed, because we must, because it is the just thing to do."

Not me. Not here. Not now. Not possible.

It can not happen to me. It can not happen in a place where I am. It can not happen at this time when we have made so much of progress. And it is just not possible.

Justice is a sense of security found in each one of us.

It is a trust that we repose in each other that in case there is any transgression on my rights and my fellow citizens are there for me. The society that I live in as well as the State is there to protect me and shall come to my aid.

In February 2014, I had gone to Khanpur Village in South Delhi to meet the family of a child who had been raped. Upon reaching the dingy by lanes of the congested village, I was not able to locate the house.

Upon asking a local shopkeeper for the address, he directed me to the house saying, "*Wo* rape *walaa ghar...*", (that house of rape).

It is, as if the entire identity of everyone in the household is only that there was a rape of someone living in it. This loss of identity, this stigmatisation and perpetual revictimisation at the hands of the society is itself the biggest disempowerment for not only the victim but also for the entire family.

I was appalled and embarrassed at the same time. We, as a society, had failed to protect the victim. Now, with such denouncement, we were adding to the trauma of the family instead of supporting them in their ordeal.

Society must discourage anything and everything that disempowers a victim. It should also make it unacceptable, with absolute strictness, any irresponsible commentary at all levels about crime and its association with power.

Even as the stark reality of crimes against women and children stares us in the face, generally we respond with denial or ignorance, or even indifference or apathy towards the victim. As a society, we mimic the ostrich that buries its head in the sand, in the face of an imminent danger.

When there is an incident right in the middle of

our backyards, in the buses, on the roads, next to malls, which are a part of our daily lives, we feel the danger. The danger that is here, and now. Yet, the anger and outrage is short lived.

I continue to come across people who could not believe that their daughter was being sexually abused in the next room while they watched television. Or their 9-year-old son is trying to lift up the skirts of his classmates and hitting their genital areas.

Above all, I have always been met with astonishment and shock when I tell people that according to government sources, one in four girls in India is a victim of child marriage, that is accepted, sanctioned and even celebrated by the society that does not understand that child marriage is nothing but an imminent child rape.

Such a celebration arises from our lack of knowledge, lack of understanding, and also in some ways the inherent desire to follow what or whom we consider powerful.

This variance in the perception of crime and the devaluation of the victim in the society is the biggest impediment to justice.

Lack of sympathy and empathy in the society and the State makes a person feel as if they have committed a mistake by reporting a crime.

If one goes to a police station and is made to wait for hours, and more often than not dissuaded from even registering the crime, then such a situation only adds to the lack of trust in the legal system, which is nothing but the representative of the society.

We continue to associate chastity of character with a sexual crime and start questioning the girl about her choices, her dressing or anything else which makes it appear that victim herself had contributed to the crime.

By holding on to such beliefs and making such statements, we make a heinous crime such as rape, a crime of power. This completely invalidates the crime and delegitimises the victim.

More unfortunate is the part where such statements are widely reported by the media and are sexualised. This encourages some publicity-hungry people to give such statements, thinking that bad publicity is good publicity.

After the horrific Nirbhaya gang rape, the self-styled guru called Asaram Bapu went on to say, "*ghalti ek taraf se nahi hoti.*" (mistake is never from one side alone)." And that if she would have called her rapists 'brothers' and pleaded with folded hands to leave her alone, she would have survived.

He was himself arrested under rape charges a few months later in 2013 under the newly formulated laws and was even convicted later. Asaram, and people like him, have hundreds of thousands of followers, who continue to have blind faith in him despite his criminal conviction.

People who speak such nonsense are still elected by us to Parliament and continue to hold important positions. Late Mr. Mulayam Singh Yadav, former Chief Minister and a stalwart in Indian politics, had famously said in a public meeting to an applause, "*Ladkiyan pehle dosti karti hain. Ladke ladki mein matbhed ho jata hai. Matbhed hone ke baad use rape ka naam detein hain. Ladko se ghaltiyan ho jaati hain. Kya rape mein phansi di jaeygi*?" (Girls first befriend boys; later, when there are differences, they cry rape. Should there be death penalty for rape?)

Such a misogynist response being acceptable in the society further adds to the fear of victim's stigmatisation. This happens to the extent that people who support criminals or who are criminals themselves are elected to democratic positions, revered, and sometimes even worshipped.

When such statements are given irresponsibly by public influencers, they have the potential to set or alter the policy or agenda discourse.

While the rapists are not facing the ignominy of their actions, the victims feel further discouraged to come forward and report.

This results in a collective societal response that often questions the victims themselves, while on the other hand, the lack of protection from threats including physical harm, lack of compensation and a process that makes the victims feel that they are on trial, all contribute to a situation with no justice for the victims.

A crime is a crime. Period.

For the society, the goal is to change our behaviour and prioritize the victim, their interests and rights; not transgressing and respecting others boundaries and rights, and taking responsibility of one's actions. It means being just towards the rights of the victims along with the rights of the accused but having zero tolerance and acceptance for crime.

A victim has already suffered a wrong that must be corrected. This is especially true if the victim is a child. The response of the immediate family, the neighbourhood, the school (if the victim is a child), the first responders, the doctors, the lawyers, the judges, and the media—all have a very important role to play in ensuring that the victim does not feel powerless in the pursuit of justice. All these have to come together to create a circle of love, empathy, trust and justice.

When there is a violation in anyone level of this circle of trust, support and safety, the other levels need to come together and complete the circle. A child's food, clothing and shelter maybe the primary responsibility of the family, but the overall protection and well-being of the child is the responsibility of the society.

*****

10 Years Later

In January 2024, while reading my morning newspaper, I was shocked. On the front page of a leading

English daily, there was a prominent news about the Madras High Court acquitting a man found in possession of child pornography on his phone.

The court in its judgement had held, "Mere searching for, or downloading child sexual abuse material or child pornography is not a crime."

The news of acquittals travels farther and wider than the news of the convictions and I am sure millions would have read it along with me.

The judgement was limiting to one section of law and had ignored other provisions of law that made this act a crime.

This is still a judgement that may be challenged and may be set aside, but what about millions who read or heard the news and who now believe that searching or downloading child sexual abuse material or child pornography is not a crime? Can we even imagine the repercussions of this in our society?

What the learned judge chose to ignore was that an act of child pornography was an act of child rape. And videotaped and the sexual assault on the child became a subject of the voyeuristic demand of the depraved minds in the society, subjecting the rape to be sold again and again with each download.

Maybe in the mind of the judge that person had not done the crime. Does this mean that a crime has not taken place? Can a judge of the High Court turn a blind eye to the fact that a child has been raped and no one is being held accountable for this crime?

This is the difference between any legal system aiming to uphold the rule of law vis-a-vis the rule of justice. If the judge had followed the spirit of justice, and the basic principles of unearthing such a crime, justice could have been served.

The two basic principles are – first, look beneath the surface; and secondly, follow the money trail. By following these two cardinal principles, maybe the money trail or the trail of downloads, it would have helped the police reach the child and maybe even save him.

The biggest violation of rights is in the denial of justice sheltered under the pretence of the rule of law.

Limiting the vision of justice to mere application of the technicalities of the law and that too, with a bias towards releasing the accused, is an act that promotes impunity, which further permeates and infiltrates in the society.

The responsibility of a crime must be affixed even if the punishment is lenient as discharge from accountability of actions promotes a tacit justification of the crime itself.

The public shame cannot be in being the victim of a crime. The ostracization, if any, has to be for the crime and not the victim.

Till we change the outlook from the "house of rape" to the "rapist *wala ghar*" (house of rapist), rapists will continue to thrive.

□

9

The fundamental right to justice

"Justice is the benchmark of a society's growth and development."

Respect for, and application of, the rule of law, and justness in actions, are the prerequisites for a society's development.

How are vulnerable citizens treated in a nation with considerable resources and rule of law, is what defines the true spirit of that nation.

Metaphorically, order or justice is the will of God.

Practically, justice is delivered through a system designed by the society — State, institutions and establishments. As the face of justice itself, the conduct of this system creates the perception of justice in society.

Justice is currently perceived as being limited to the rule of law. This creates the notion of justice delivery as being mostly dependent upon the existing laws and their interpretation and enforcement.

However, the mere existence of laws, police, courts or other such institutional mechanisms is not a guarantee of justice by itself.

Laws may be unjust, they may be inadequate, they may not even exist. Policies or laws may not be implemented or enforced or they may be enforced in such mechanical ways, or with such long delays that they render their implementation meaningless.

This also results in a lackadaisical attitude in society towards the rule of law and its application. This attitude further promotes impunity, desensitisation and an abdication of collective responsibility.

All these issues create a vicious circle where each is a cause as well as a consequence of the other. This vicious circle can only be broken by taking a holistic approach of a systemic overhaul towards the rule of justice.

The Constitution creates the normative order and system of governance in a society. Therefore, any assurance of justice needs to arise from a constitutional guarantee as a right itself.

In most Constitutions across the world, 'justice' or 'access to justice' is an inherent interpretation found in various other rights but not defined as an explicit right by itself.

In India, justice is limited to the Preamble to the Indian Constitution that starts with a solemn promise to secure "...Justice, social, economic and political..." The Preamble also does not explicitly mention legal justice, which is assumed to be a part of various other fundamental rights along with social justice, economic justice and political justice.

Even 'access to justice' was never explicitly included in the original Constitution of India. Article 39A was inserted in the Directive Principles of State Policy wherein the State is duty-bound to provide legal aid and access to justice, in 1977, through a constitutional amendment. This limited inclusion has proven to be not enough towards the end goal of securing and ensuring justice for all.

Currently, some of the ingredients of justice in the Indian Constitution are, legal aid, access to justice or speedy trials. As justice itself is not seen as an end goal, it has been limited primarily to these three interpretations.

All these issues prevent the rule of law from translating into the rule of justice.

In any constitution, justice should be the core principle and an inherent right from which every other right follows.

Justice as a Fundamental Right, that is not only an

interpretation found in judicial orders, not only limited to a value or promise as enshrined in the Preamble to Constitution, or a duty of the State under Article 39A, rather is the basis of the notion of our society, and from which all the other fundamental rights, duties and laws follow, and are enforced.

The smallest outcome of this would be an acceptance and assurance of all rights of the victims of crimes, their reparation, reintegration in mainstream society, and the trial process not being limited to crime and punishment alone. If right to fair trial is for an accused, the gaurantee of legal justice also must be for the victim.

In the cases where the culprits are not convicted, those cases would not become dead. If a crime is committed, even if there is an acquittal, the case continues (or is reinvestigated) with the State having to ascertain that a crime does not go unpunished, and an acquittal does not mean the closure of a case.

Where the laws are inadequate to ensure justice they are promptly formulated or amended; where they are not being interpreted or enforced towards justice for the victims, there is accountability of inactions; omission and delays, and laws are understood and acknowledged as instruments for the delivery of justice.

Another outcome would be an enhanced understanding that justice is not being limited to only citizens but all that exists within the State. It does not only mean access to justice. Such access to social, economic, political or legal rights is only a part of this overall notion and value.

An inherent question is whether justice is a responsibility or a duty of the State, or an inalienable right of the citizen. If it is the latter, then a lack or denial of it is State's responsibility.

This notion of justice being defined as a duty itself limits its application as a right. This must change now from the citizen being a recipient of justice as a State responsibility or duty, to the citizen being a holder of justice as a fundamental right.

This conversion from being a Directive Principle of State Policy into an explicitly laid down Fundamental Right to Justice shall then, eventually, seep into governance, institutions of the State machinery, as well as the citizenry, with each fulfilling their roles and catering to their responsibilities as service to the people.

Society accessing and practicing justice as a right would result in an enhanced vision, empowerment and a sense of responsibility, accountability and deterrence for everyone.

Justice as a fundamental right will have an immense impact on the lives of ordinary citizens with these obligations becoming enforceable - third parties or citizens can make the State deliver what is due to individuals or groups.

While the Constitution is the custodian of the State, its democracy and its citizenry, it also needs to transcend into the consciousness and conscience of the society. When the citizen is the holder of rights and not a subject of the benevolence of the State, the Fundamental Right to Justice is the fulcrum for balance in society and its consciousness.

As the true spirit of a nation is defined by the justice that exists in it, the only assurance of this spirit can be through the Constitution mandating a Fundamental Right to Justice.

*****

India is well on its way to emerging as a global super power. The Constitution of 1950, written and adopted immediately after independence, laid the basis of where we have reached today.

The time is here to have a collective goal of humanity for the 22nd century and a 'Vision 2100' for India as a nation. A vision that ensures equality, freedom, security and dignity for all its citizens, with the Fundamental Right to Justice as its cornerstone.

Now, WE, THE PEOPLE OF INDIA, have to find the will, and fight for this vision and hope.

□

In one epoch, God observed it all and smiled.

In all His creations, from stars to planets and constellations, and all the forms of life, in all the possible multiverses, the cycle of life continued and all, or most, was in order.

It was just.

The stars followed gravity, and gravity was itself love because it brought one thing closer to another. It was also just, and in order, because it kept everything at exactly the right distance from each other.

Where the order was violated, one infringed and transgressed on the space and the right of another, and created black holes where one would subsume the other.

Sometimes, these black holes could be amongst stars, and sometimes amongst people.

When the desire of one exceeded one's need and the order was broken because of one's greed, one infringed on another.

Of all the creations of God, most were just and some were on a journey of being just.

We as humans, are but a tiny speck in the life of time, and follow the path of being just. This is our journey.

Someday, this collective consciousness will arise, and in a proximate space and time, we will find the path of equilibrium, of being just and just being, of 'Justivism'.

Someday, soon enough, amidst the people who love, and the people who love being just, we will find amongst ourselves a 'JUSTIVIST'!

□

Acknowledgements

My friends and family, who have walked with me every step of the way, and without whose trust, faith, love, teachings and support, I would not be anywhere.

All my teachers who invariably struggled to teach me, and yet remained patient. Especially, Mrs. Reeta Kaale and Mr. Ajit Singh, my middle school teachers, whose unflinching faith in me, and encouragement despite my repeated failures, play a large part in whatever I do and wherever I go.

Ramesh Gupta *ji*, who was my first introduction as a young boy of 14, to law and its nuances, and later, as a senior lawyer taught me the value of 'there is always another chance', and 'a lawyer loses only when they lose hope and give up'.

Dr. Lajpat Rai (late) nana *ji*, who pushed me to study law.

Teachers at the Faculty of law, Delhi University, especially Mr. Anupam Singh, who got me to think on the ideals of justice beyond laws.

R.S. Chaurasia *ji* (Comrade), whose resilience, dedication and commitment to the poor and vulnerable, exemplifies the spirit of social justice, and who, in my humble opinion, is one of the last remaining saints on earth.

All my colleagues, who exemplify the fight of, and fight for the vulnerable every day, and whose love and commitment for the cause of justice, is an inspiration to emulate.

Rajat Kumar, Vijay Singh, Danish Raza, Owain James & Priyanka *ji* for their remarkable patience during seemingly endless reviews and edits of this book.

The police officer, who played with me and ensured I got milk, bread and biscuits as an 8-year-old, detained along with my parents during a public march against Sati. And all other police officers, lawyers, prosecutors and judges, who continue to show every day that the most important real heroes are the ones in khaki, or in black or white, doing a lot of little things that make this world just right!